MIND *your* BODY
WORK *your* SOUL

CLARE **STROCKBINE**

Liguori
LIGUORI, MISSOURI

Imprimi Potest:
Harry Grile, CSsR, Provincial
Denver Province, The Redemptorists

Published by Liguori Publications
Liguori, Missouri 63057

To order, call 800-325-9521
www.liguori.org

Library of Congress Cataloging-in-Publication Data
Strockbine, Clare.
  Mind your body, work your soul / by Clare Strockbine. — First Edition.
    pages cm
  Includes bibliographical references.
  1. Health—Religious aspects—Catholic Church. 2. Catholic Church—Doctrines.
I. Title.
  BX1795.H4S77 2013
  248.4—dc23

                                                                2013010675

p ISBN: 978-0-7648-2245-2
e ISBN: 978-0-7648-6834-4

Liguori Publications, a nonprofit corporation, is an apostolate of The Redemptorists. To learn more about The Redemptorists, visit Redemptorists.com.

Printed in the United States of America
17 16 15 14 13 / 5 4 3 2 1
First Edition

CONTENTS

ACKNOWLEDGMENTS

I had a dear friend in graduate school who used a wonderful visual aid to show the importance of sharing our stories. He would take a big jar and fill it with a number of pebbles, representing all the different responsibilities, tasks, stressors—the "things" with which we consume our days. He would stuff as many stones as possible in the jar until not one more pebble could fit. Then he would take a cup of coffee and pour it into the jar. The coffee found its way around, under, above, and between the pebbles; no matter how many pebbles were in the jar, there was always room for the coffee. He used this to communicate to young college first-years that no matter how full our days are and how many things are on our to-do list, we always have time to share a cup of coffee with another—to share stories.

I have been incredibly blessed to be the recipient of the stories of so many amazing individuals. Without their stories—without their guidance, support, and encouragement—I would not be where I am today and this book would not be a reality. I never imagined that my experiences would end up manifesting themselves in a piece such as this, and I still sometimes wonder how Christy Hicks had the foresight to see it all. I am grateful she did, and I hope and pray that by sharing my story and asking some questions, others will have the courage not only to share their stories but to challenge the status quo in which we often find ourselves, both personally and as a global community.

I would be remiss not to mention a few people who have been instrumental in my journey and are, in many ways, the reason I am healthy enough today to write this book. I need to thank my editor, Erin Cartaya, for visioning and exploring with me as this all came to fruition (and her immeasurable patience with my struggle to meet deadlines!) and Liguori Publications for taking a chance on a young new author. To "Uncle" Paul Ginnetty for making the time for me when I know you are bursting at the seams with your own tasks—thank you. Julie Lupien, you have been a source of more support for me than you can imagine, and your abundant gifts to me have been instrumental in my arrival at this point. I wouldn't be in this were it not for you, and we're in it together.

I am grateful for my family, as you have perhaps accustomed yourselves to not questioning my decisions and life choices that are often seen as quite countercultural by Western society's standards. For my dad for sending me limitless advice and encouragement on physical fitness, health, and life in general. For my loved ones in Ecuador, my Rostro communities, and those with whom I had the privilege of walking those dirt streets—*ya saben*. For Melissa and the Casa Ritmo family, thank you for giving me a way to survive for a year, not to mention incredible support and friendship.

To Robin, thank you for being one of the great reasons I love my job and for your unfailing desire to be better. Mara, thank you for continuously inviting me—*gracias, señor, gracias*! For Terri Boggess, who is a shining example of what health in all of its dimensions should be. If I can become half the woman you are, I will consider myself a success. *Le agradezco a mi esposo y mejor amigo, Yonatan—por siempre apoyarme, comprenderme, e amarme, y por la fuerza para seguir a Dios en este camino juntos.* I am so thankful to have landed at St. Mary's and for the Marianist family; understanding and supporting (literally) the connection between our physical and spiritual selves is not always common. Thank you for being the visionaries that Chaminade calls us to be in a world that desperately needs compassion, faith, and justice.

Finally, for Pop-Pop: among a long list of other invaluable insights you shared, for asking me every time we spoke for twenty-seven years if I took my vitamins and said my prayers to the Blessed Mother. You offered a vision of complete health that is unparalleled. You are missed.

I hold all of you—and so many who go here unmentioned—in prayer and in gratitude. Thank you for being a part of my journey, and may you continue to share your stories and change lives as you have mine. May you all be well.

"JUST" HEALTH

I have always loved baseball. I was raised as a pretty strong Mets fan (as a child, thanks to my dad, I truly believed the "Stankees" was the official American League baseball team in New York). I loved watching games, collecting baseball cards, proclaiming my adoration of Dwight Gooden and Darryl Strawberry (though my love for the latter dissipated with his involvement in drugs and subsequent signing with the Yankees).

The days we spent at Shea Stadium were glorious. I also remember seeing various players make the Sign of the Cross before stepping up to bat or folding their hands in what appeared to be prayer as they sat on the bench awaiting the start of the game. As a child, I didn't think much of it. It wasn't until I was much older and involved in sports and important games myself that I came to appreciate why some players would have been praying before coming to the plate. However, let's be clear on one thing: my mediocre playing was far from producing the stress these guys must have been under. Even then, though, my comprehension of that connection was limited. It took much more living, much more failure, much more experience, and much more opportunity for growth in my own personhood to understand the what, why, and how of that connection between the physical and spiritual being.

These physical and spiritual parts of our being, these inward and outward manifestations of our heart and soul, are key components of our existence. The way we are on the inside and on the outside, the way we care for ourselves, and the value we place on these aspects in many ways dictate how healthy we are, how

7

much we can and do give to the world. Are we at our best so we can give our best? If we look at the different aspects of our lives—our physical being, our spirituality, our interactions with other persons, our interactions with the world at large, the way we think, act, pray, speak—how healthy can we say we are?

Martin Luther King, Jr., said, "Peace is not the absence of conflict, but the presence of justice." Similarly, health is not the absence of illness, but the presence of justice—yes, you read that correctly, *the presence of justice.* How can this be? What do health and justice have to do with each other? One relates to an annual physical exam, to medications (or lack thereof), to engaging in physical activity, to not sniffling or coughing up a lung. The other has to do with theories and activism, with standing up for one's beliefs and creating a world of equality and fair distribution of resources, with analyzing and employing the principles of Catholic social teaching and striving for recognition of the dignity of all peoples and pieces of creation—right?

Well, not exactly. There's a bit more to it than that.

Justice, as we know it in our Catholic faith tradition, means being in right relationship, that is, finding, creating, and pursuing the presence of right relationships with God, self, others, and creation. Many experts characterize health in six dimensions: physical, social, emotional, environmental, mental, and spiritual. To be complete, to be in right relationship, to be healthy, we need to take responsibility for caring for ourselves, but we also need the help of others to do it well. Let's look at each of these dimensions a bit more closely.

PHYSICAL HEALTH

To be physically healthy often means being void of illness, but it goes a bit further; we must look at various aspects of life. The U.S. Surgeon General recommends at least thirty minutes of exercise a day for all people over the age of two. (See NSCA's *Essentials of Personal Training,* p. 398.) Being physically active—intentionally—each day helps us keep moving, our muscles working, our blood pumping. It can assist in injury and disease prevention (such as osteoporosis, arthritis, and hypertension). For those who suffer from being overweight or obese, exercising each day can help them lose weight and obtain/increase physical fitness. Being physically active and being physically fit are two different things. Physical activity merely denotes movement of some kind; physical fitness is more about being in good shape, possessing levels of muscular and cardiovascular strength and endurance—the ability to successfully complete higher levels of (often skilled) physical activity.

Being physically healthy also takes into account one's diet and habits. For example, if you consume extreme levels of sugar or fat or smoke a pack of cigarettes a day, more than likely your physical health is, or will be, compromised. Poor sleep patterns affect one's energy and activity levels (not to mention one's metabolism and links to weight management). Studies show that those with nutritionally imbalanced diets, heavy smokers and/or drinkers, and those whose daily routines lack physical activity often suffer from health complications.

Now, if you are sitting there thinking, *Well, I don't exercise intentionally at all* or *I've been trying to quit smoking for the past decade and just haven't been able to kick the habit,* this isn't meant to make you feel inferior or worthless. Despite my involvement in sports during most of my childhood and adolescence, I have struggled with weight my entire life and have been through stages of obesity. I used to be a smoker, and during my college years I enjoyed more than my fair share of libations (after I was of age, of course). Sometimes all of this information and insight into physical health can sound preachy—and impossible, depending on where we're sitting. That is certainly not my intention. I offer it as someone for whom it didn't come naturally and who has had to work for where I am now, as someone who had to learn willpower and self-discipline and make some really hard choices at various times in my life. My point is, it's *possible* to change our lifestyle—but not only do we have to want it, I would also argue that we'll only succeed at changing our lifestyle permanently and getting ourselves on a path to good physical health when we look at all aspects of wellness and get ourselves in check in all dimensions.

Think about your daily routine. Do you make a point of going for a walk, getting to the gym a few times a week, playing a game of pickup with some friends at the park, taking advantage of being outside on a sunny Saturday? When you invite someone over for dinner, what's your go-to recipe? Are you getting a variety of vegetables, fruits, and protein in there, or do you head straight for the chicken-fried steak ingredients at the grocery store? Do you get together with friends at the park or for a walk around the lake or is it always a matter of "Let's get together for a drink"? Do your children watch television or get on the computer for hours on end when they get home from school or do you make them spend some time outside and limit their sedentary activities? What do your portions look like when you sit down to a meal? Do you eat until you are no longer hungry or do you eat until you are full?

Physical health is a vital component of our overall being and requires an awareness of one's body and its functions and a commitment to exercise, diet, sleep, and good habits of daily life. Conquering and preventing illness, engaging in daily exercise, pushing oneself to be physically fit, knowledge of how food and behavior affect the capability of our bodies to perform as necessary are all part of establishing and maintaining physical health, and we must indeed give it due importance.

We strive for a relationship with our body that promotes energy and the ability to function well. We yearn to be, look, and feel healthy—to relish in a place and space within ourselves where are bodies are capable of the daily routine and the occasional tough physical challenge. We search for the place of justice, of right relationship—where who we are and what we can do meet and gel together quite nicely. Yet the physical aspect of health is not the only one we must examine and certainly is not a solitary piece of the health puzzle.

SOCIAL HEALTH

Our relationships with others in many ways can help to define who we are. As human beings, we need one another—we need human contact, we need friends and family, we need to understand our role as it relates to our chosen social circle, to our immediate surroundings, and to our larger global community. Though we all vary on the introvert/extrovert scale, ultimately we need other human beings. We may not necessarily gain our greatest renewal of energy from being around others nor feel the most comfortable in a crowd of strangers, but we were created to be social beings. Scripture gives us examples of community, of how we are created to be and care for one another. Let's take a look at one of the greatest examples of being socially healthy, which comes from Peter's speech at Pentecost:

> "They devoted themselves to the teaching of the apostles and to the communal life, to the breaking of the bread and to the prayers. Awe came upon everyone, and many wonders and signs were done through the apostles. All who believed were together and had all things in common; they would sell their property and possessions and divide them among all according to each one's need. Every day they devoted themselves to meeting together in the temple area and to

breaking bread in their homes. They ate their meals with exultation and sincerity of heart, praising God and enjoying favor with all the people. And every day the Lord added to their number those who were being saved" (Acts 2:42–47).

As a community of believers, we are called to gather, to break bread, to shared prayer, to distribute resources as needed, to join together with glad and sincere hearts.

Maintaining this sense of social health requires that we learn to be in relationship with others—to forgo always putting ourselves first, to contemplate the other, to recognize the dignity and worth of each and every individual from every walk of life. It requires putting ourselves in the shoes of the other and trying to understand the perspectives of those with whom we come in contact. But it also calls us to learn from the world around us—from our sisters and brothers thousands of miles away who may speak a language and live in a culture vastly different from any we have ever known or may ever experience.

My grandfather was a character—and the greatest man I have ever known. One of the many things that made him so wonderful was that he never shied away from imparting his wisdom upon his grandchildren, or anyone else for that matter. Many of his sayings still run through my mind on a daily basis, though we lost him a few years ago. Anyone in my family would be able to share with you one of his most common quotes, "Choose your friends wisely."

There is a lot of truth in his words—whom we choose to associate with plays a huge part in who we are and who we become. The ideal is to surround ourselves with other "believers"—those who share our vision for a greater world; those who aim to share bread, prayer, and resources; those who encourage us to grow and be healthy and who challenge us to constantly strive to be better, do more, live more authentically. If we are living according to the example Scripture gives us, the idea is simple: We, the community of believers, are living in such a beautiful, true, and just manner that others cannot help but be attracted to our lifestyle. And so our community grows—crossing nations, crossing cultural boundaries, crossing language barriers, crossing religious, economic, and societal divides.

Being socially healthy means we strive to be in the world in such a way that we exude respect and love for the other; it also means, on a very basic level, that we understand when we need time alone, when we need space and quiet, and to attend to those needs. You may have often heard the quote, especially within any sort of helping profession, "You cannot give from what you do not have." (This advice has roots in the Roman Catholic Church. It was introduced in Latin, "*Nemo potest dare quod non habet*," as part of emphasizing basic truths in the formation for priests.)

If we are tired and drained and do not take the time to rejuvenate and find balance and joy in our own lives, to meet our own needs, we will not be able to treat others with joy or walk with them in their journey toward wholeness. This is not to say we are always whole, always happy, or ever perfect. But we must meet our own needs if we are to meet the needs of others whom we serve and with whom we walk. Finding a balance between the time we need alone—in reflection, thought, prayer, and so forth—and the time we spend with others is going to vary with each person. We must find time to relax with friends, have meaningful conversations, share meals with those who are close to us and with whom we feel a friendship. We must also challenge ourselves and those around us to analyze and pay attention not only to the relationship we have with people who surround us daily, but our need to value and care for the relationship we have with people we don't know simply by being our human brothers and sisters.

As some of us may be more introverted and others more extroverted, these ways of rejuvenating and finding balance are going to look different and be more specific depending on the person. As such, not only must we know ourselves well enough to know where we fall and how we best interact with and get energy from other people, but we also need to respect how those who are close to us need others as well.

In my late twenties, I lived in an intentional Christian community with individuals who were all far more extroverted than I am. For the most part, they got their energy from being around semi-large groups of people in loud bars, having a drink and being out and about. I, on the other hand, desperately needed to sit in a quiet space and share intimate conversation with just one or two people. It took a great deal of time and energy (and several ups and downs) to attempt to find a balance within our community—a place where we could understand and try to meet one another's needs. Though we tried, we never quite found the "right" space. Interestingly, the longer I lived with them, the more introverted I became. This was not a bad thing, but it certainly was unexpected. My relationship in this community changed and shaped me into a different person. Although I didn't necessarily make significant headway in my place in this community, by focusing and reflecting on this aspect of my health, my interactions with them led me to a deeper understanding of the relationship I had with myself. Though more introverted, I didn't become less "socially healthy"; I just learned more about who I am, what I need, and the types of personalities and people I need to be around to maintain my health.

What do you need to maintain this balance in your life, to be healthy in relationship with others? Do you need time alone, time with one trusted friend, time out and about with a large social network? How do you interact with others? How do you help others maintain their sense of self and health? Who is close to you, and how do you help to meet their needs and encourage their social health? What are some concrete ways in which you seek to balance your needs in relationship with others?

EMOTIONAL HEALTH

One of the greatest factors in our emotional state of being is stress. We have all experienced stressful situations at some point in our lives. How we cope with stress and our ability to see the bigger picture can say a lot about how emotionally healthy we are. As we find outlets for stress that contribute to our overall health and well-being—prayer, journaling, exercise, talking with friends, watching a movie—we learn to cope with stress. As we learn to do this, we learn more about ourselves and grow in our ability to maintain a sense of contentment, a sense of balance, and the ability to put things in perspective. We can laugh at the small things and give attention to the big things when necessary.

Our emotional health also has much to do with how we see and feel about ourselves. Especially in our (Western) society today, media, magazines, and television all tell us we should look a certain way, obtain a certain level of education, and achieve certain salaries and "status." In many ways, this strips us of the opportunity to develop and contribute our individual gifts to the world. We may have a passion for painting or dance or a certain sport, but if we don't fit a certain body type or have certain letters after our name, we will not be "successful"—which for many in our society means we will not contribute significantly to our world. I'll delve into this more later, but ultimately we need to do what we love with conviction and belief. When we are true to our gifts and to ourselves, more often than not we feel good about ourselves—independently of how a certain sector of society judges us.

A few years ago I picked up the practice of social salsa dancing. Having recently moved to a new city, I knew only one acquaintance.

She was an amazing dancer, and when she was on the dance floor, one could clearly see the joy in her face; she was in a different place when she danced, and it was evident. She invited me to go dancing one night, and I remember thinking, *I want to feel that joy. I want to get lost in that movement, in the music, to be outside of myself experiencing that joy.* So I started taking some lessons and gradually learned the basic steps, though I felt very unsure of myself and hesitated to go out on the dance floor. I felt as though I didn't *look* like a dancer.

As I continued to go out dancing socially, I noticed an amazing factor: Women who salsa dance are *all so different.* If you've ever been out to a salsa club, you know what I mean; these women move across the dance floor with the lightness of a floating feather, and they are all different shapes and sizes. Some women are incredibly short, some are incredibly overweight, some have very wide hips, some are tall and lanky—and they all move with remarkable grace; they free themselves to the music. I felt empowered by witnessing the dancing of these women. I realized I don't need to look a certain way or have a certain percentage of body fat; there is a place for everyone. We are created in God's image and likeness—similar to the church community we strive to create. On the dance floor, all are welcome and encouraged to move to the music, just as you are.

We have all been made and crafted differently—short, tall; big-boned, small-boned; with the ability to dance, maybe to sing, or to understand complex mathematical problems. We all have different gifts. The important part is to be true to ourselves—to strive for overall health in all of its dimensions—to see ourselves and one another for the remarkable gift that is each individual person. To recognize our own gifts, talents, and passions (and, yes, our shortcomings) is to feel empowered and joyful in the unique person we are and to find that place of emotional balance.

ENVIRONMENTAL HEALTH

One aspect of health often overlooked is what experts have identified as environmental health. It sounds broad, and perhaps you're thinking, *I recycle. Obviously, I'm fine in this aspect,* or *I can't stand pollution and am aware of my carbon footprint. Environmental health...check.* This dimension of health encompasses an awareness of how one uses natural resources, cares for the earth, and respects creation. However, when we think of our environment, we also need to think about it as, very simply, our surroundings—not just our ecological surroundings but the people and everyone's access to equal opportunities.

Think about the environment in which you grew up. Were you able to play outside without fear of kidnapping, assault, or witnessing drug deals? Could you run barefoot through the lawn of your childhood home, or did your front door lead out to a dirt road that might have been latent with trash, broken glass, and bacteria? After you had been running around playing tag or hide-and-seek and came inside hot and thirsty, did you have access to clean drinking water? Could you breathe the air outside without coughing and gagging from pollution and dust?

All people should have the opportunity to run, play, and engage in physical activity without fear of safety, without discrimination, without judgment. I participated in sports all my life; would that have been different had I not grown up in a middle-class suburb of Long Island? Would I have had the same access to activity and freedom if I had grown up in an identified war zone or in specific gang territory in the inner city? I was fortunate to have grown up in a home where my family gave me opportunities to join the church softball league and take swim lessons; my mom washed my uniforms, my grandfather dropped me off at swim practice, and my dad came to my track meets. My grade school planted trees every Earth Day, and my Girl Scout troop participated in service projects to beautify neighborhoods through trash pickup and planting flowers. Where would I have been if I had been born into a socioeconomic situation that did not enable my childhood to be this way? Would my environment have been one that spoke of health?

Peter Klavora, in his work *Foundations of Kinesiology*, reminds us that "the World Health Organization's definition of health is 'the capacity to lead a satisfying life, fulfill ambitions, and accommodate change'" (p. 318). At this point in our global reality, does each and every person have the ability to be healthy according to this definition? Can a child born into a small, undeveloped village in West Africa, where many children don't *start* school (much less *finish* school), have the opportunity to say he wants to be a lawyer when he grows up and make it happen? Can children in Ecuador, whose rate of malnutrition hovers around 26 percent for those under the age of five, lead a satisfying life?

Awareness of the dimension of environmental health demands that we understand the need to recycle, to address the phenomenon of slash-and-burn techniques and the ramifications it has for our ecosystems (particularly on our rain forests) to challenge oil and gas companies on the effects of fracking. Paying attention to environmental health also calls us to task in questioning the situation into which each person is born. Do all of us, as human beings, have access to growing up in a healthy environment?

How do I care for the environment and creation; how do I create an environment that reaps justice and equality, that allows children to play and dream and invent and parents to not fear letting their kids ride their bike to the neighbor's house?

MENTAL HEALTH

As we think of health, it may be inherent for most of us to assume challenge—becoming and staying healthy is certainly a challenge for most of us. But accepting challenge with a willingness to learn and embrace and grow is, in and of itself, descriptive of yet another aspect of health—our mental health. Mental health can and does relate to chemical brain balances, our developmental capabilities, varying illnesses, and so forth. But one can be mentally unhealthy in a plethora of ways. Do you see challenges in life as opportunities for growth, to learn? Do you challenge yourself to take on new projects, new ventures, discover new ways of thinking? Do you engage in activities and conversations that stimulate the mind and cause you to explore new perspectives and approaches? Do you let yourself be influenced by the opinions of others, let yourself get talked out of something you know in your heart and mind God is calling you to do?

It happens to us all. I was nineteen when I met motivational Chuck. I was halfway through my college career and was preparing to go on a weeklong service immersion trip to Ecuador. It was run through the campus ministry department of my university, and the application process really was entered into and treated as a discernment. I knew God was calling me to Ecuador—it was strong on my heart; I truly felt it was a calling and that I was going to be changed in ways I couldn't then begin to imagine, getting ready to receive whatever gift and task to which God was calling me. Isn't it amazing, that feeling when you know, so strongly rooted in your heart, that this *(fill in the blank with the opportunity that applies to your life…marriage, new job, pregnancy)* is absolutely where and to what God is calling you? It's an incredibly powerful, overwhelming, all-encompassing experience.

Part of our preparation included some fundraising to help cover the costs of our trip, so a friend and I set up outside a grocery store one afternoon to do just that. We displayed a piece of cardboard with the words "Please help send us to Ecuador" written on it and maybe two pamphlets and a few pictures from previous university-sponsored groups who had gone. (Thinking about it now, I realize we looked like a pretty shady operation, but at the time I'm sure we thought we were about to gather all the money we would need in a four-hour span that day. It's OK, you can chuckle at the young idealism.) That day is forever etched in my memory.

We encountered some tough moments that day. We had more than a few people snicker at us; many looked at us with faces that said, "Yeah, right"; and one man ripped us apart. He was older, a veteran, who surely carried his own life experience and baggage and hurt with him and who had probably seen more than his fair share of suffering and pain. For whatever reason, we were the recipients of his cynicism and critical eye that day. He told us we were fools, that there were far too many people in our own country who needed help (a fair statement and another topic of conversation that could go on far too long), that we were traitors for going overseas to "help" others when we were "Americans" and should stay here and help, that we would make no difference there to anyone, and how could our parents and school support such ridiculousness.

Needless to say, my friend and I were crushed—we questioned why in the world were we going to Ecuador? Why would God call us to something that was so wrong, that people thought was ridiculous, that society claimed was a waste of our time and money? Have you ever had a similar experience? You are so gung ho about something you know in your heart to be right. You feel that "tug," and you just know God is calling you to something that, assumingly, will be amazing. You have no other way to describe it than, "I just *know* this is right. I have no idea why and I don't know what's in store and there is a much bigger plan out there for me than I can begin to dream and I am clueless as to where all this will lead, but I have to do it. I know this is right." And then, lo and behold, some overrated, overcautious, overcritical, far too play-it-safe voice (be it in your own heart or that of someone else) tells you, "You can't do that. It's not *normal*. People just don't *do* that sort of thing. Don't be a fool." Have you had this experience? It sure is a slap in the face.

Fortunately for my friend and me, along came motivational Chuck. We were just about ready to pack up when he walked by and lingered for a moment at our table of pamphlets and handmade sign. He asked what we would be doing in Ecuador, and we shared with him the goals of our faith-based immersion, of learning and striving to understand how another part of the world lived, of wanting to understand this human bond we shared with people who grew up in a reality so radically different from our own. He listened, nodded, and calmly said, "Don't leave. I'll help you out when I'm finished shopping."

A bit later he came back to our table (much to our surprise). He talked with us a little bit and verbalized his support and encouragement. He then handed us a twenty-dollar bill and said something I've never forgotten: "The more people tell you you're crazy for doing what you're passionate about, the more you know you're on the right track."

The word *crazy* is often negatively (and quite inappropriately and without couth or compassion) associated with mental illness. But believing in our call and trusting in what God calls us to, knowing we can seek out and embrace new opportunities and adventures and having the courage to do so despite what society tells us is normal may be "crazy," but it gives us the chance to witness grace. This is all part of being mentally sound and healthy. Our ability to identify possibilities for ourselves; consider various options, choices, and alternatives when making a decision; the know-how to put oneself in another's shoes; our capability to handle stressful situations—all come into play when looking at overall mental health.

Constantly striving to become a better person, to learn more, to give more and grow more, to not be complacent in who we are or with the world's status quo, and to recognize who we are both as individuals and as members of a larger community are all part and parcel of maintaining a healthy state of mind. Seeing ourselves as magnificent creations of the Divine, as children of and gifts from God, of taking advantage of the opportunities God places in our lives, and honoring the beauty that lies not just in others around us but in ourselves—are all a big piece of being mentally healthy.

SPIRITUAL HEALTH

I'm a lover of quotes—quotes from all sorts of authors on numerous topics from the remarkably profound to the most sincerely simple. In all my reading and studying and listening—all of which I feel I've done in decently large quantities—I have yet to find one that seems to accurately and poignantly express the necessity of one's spirituality in terms of being overall healthy. And let's take a minute to be clear on something: spirituality is not limited to "I believe in God." For Catholics, belief and trust in God are a part of our spirituality—but it is so much more than that. Spirituality is faith, is trust, is surrendering to God's will, is discernment and fulfillment of vocation, is participating in a faith community, is awareness of a holy Presence within and beyond any human. Spirituality is a longing for the kingdom to be among us and working very hard to make it happen—even if we never see it during our time on earth. Remember that whole "prophets of a future not our own" line often attributed to Archbishop Romero? Bishop Ken Untener was on to something when he wrote that prayer. It is a tangible "both/and," a way of living and being in the world that is consistent with the Gospel—that is, with the example of Jesus. Spirituality—faith—at its best is justice; it is wholeness and health.

Being spiritually healthy doesn't boil down to "Do you go to church on Sunday?" If only it were that easy! Rather, spiritual health is about listening to the voice of God in your life as you discover your passion, and then using your passion to serve the world for the greater good in light of your faith. Spiritual health is about the journey toward wholeness; a seeking of the Divine in ourselves and others amidst our raw humanity; not just an acceptance but an *embrace* of the unique role to which God calls each of us on this earth. This way of being healthy denotes a lived understanding and an implementation of a faith that, while not always easy and very often full of challenges, struggles, and sometimes unpleasant or uncomfortable opportunities for growth, constantly leaves room for grace and lets the Holy Spirit work her magic. (Sounds somewhat familiar, right? These dimensions of health all flow into and out of one another—there's unbelievable interconnectedness.)

What is your relationship with God looking like these days? How do you best relate to God…as a mother? Father? All-knowing creator? Friend? Authority figure? How do you listen for God's voice in your life? Do you feel God speaks to you most through other people, through nature, through quiet moments in prayer? How do you most make yourself open to what God has to say to you? Understanding more fully this complex relationship between humanity and God is part of our soul-searching, part of our journey of being. What ways do you use to open your ears and heart to the whispers of God's voice?

The Jesuits have two key words that give some form and structure to the journey of spiritual health and the way in which we experience this relationship with God: consolation and desolation. These words are most commonly used in the process of discernment—that is, trying to hear and understand where God is calling you, where your personal gifts meet the world's needs. How often have you stopped to really, truly ponder that? What are your own unique gifts? What do you do well? What do you like to do? What skills and talents and natural abilities do you bring to the table that differ from others in the seats next to you? What, specifically, were you created for? What is the state of the world right now, and how can you use your gifts and your passions to help improve it?

Desolation (or a state of being unhealthy in the spiritual context) is the space in which we are turned away from God; we feel cut off from community, we are exhausted, we have little to no greater vision. In contrast, consolation draws us closer to God, improves our relationship with God, and allows our gifts to be put to good use in service to others. When we are spiritually healthy, we find ourselves in this place of consolation. Here we have energy; we are attentive to God's presence in our lives; we are aware of the joys and sorrows of others and are able to offer genuine compassion; we are living for others and have hearts that are full, generous, and joyful.

As we grow toward and (hopefully) attain spiritual health, we find ourselves in right relationship with God and—well, would you look at this—in right relationship with self, creation, and others, as we have just identified the components of being spiritually healthy focusing us outward.

So much of this idea of health is about knowing ourselves—as we are, as we yearn to be; as we relate to others and allow others to relate to us; as we know God and as we open ourselves to God's speaking to us. As we look at health through these different lenses, through these varying dimensions that all play a part in making up one overarching umbrella of health and wholeness, maybe this doesn't sound so off the mark after all. There just might be a correlation here between health and the presence of justice; there just might be a way to search out and achieve a place of right relationship.

IF NOT, CAN I GET MY MONEY BACK?

Can you imagine what life would be like if we could snap our fingers and make something happen? "I want to visit Bali." Snap! I'm there. "I'd like $1,000." Snap! Cash is in my hand. "I want to be able to hike up that mountain, never fight with my husband, and have zero doubt in my mind at all times that God is everywhere and all will be well simply because I know I'm following God's call for me in life without question or concern." Yeah, I'd say that would be nice. If only making our way to this whole "right relationship" thing were that easy.

* * *

There are a lot of "quick fix" scams out there. On any day of the week we can walk into a grocery store and between the magazines at the checkout line and the vitamin aisle, we will likely encounter more products and "easy" methods to "slim down fast," "boost your metabolism," "lose ten pounds," "look half your age" (you get the idea) than we can count on two hands. Turn on the television anytime after midnight and get sucked in by the infomercials, and forget it—we're in trouble (and likely to be taken for six easy payments of $19.99; after all, it's new and improved). We're constantly being bombarded with these advertisements of what we can use to look "better"—younger, thinner, more muscular, have shinier hair, and so forth. On our good days, we might recognize that this is all strategic advertising and an attempt to coax us into buying some product that will never, ever work. (We often neglect the asterisk and fine print—"Results will vary with each individual.

Must be combined with a reduction of calories in daily diet and regular exercise.") So why is it that at times we *all* let ourselves get drawn in to this marketing ploy?

Now, I consider myself a fairly well-educated person. I've earned two degrees, multiple certifications, and continuing-education credits. I teach undergraduate courses at a university. I've been very lucky to have some pretty quality education come my way. This makes me no better and no worse than another person on this earth. But I would hope that it would help me—especially considering one of my degrees is in Communications with a focus on public relations and advertising—to be a bit more skeptical of advertising scams, of bogus-sounding products, of fad diets. Am I skeptical? Absolutely…on my good days. But Lord knows, not all our days are good, no matter who we are or how educated.

I have taken dietary supplement pills to decrease my appetite and increase my metabolism. Did they work? (Do I actually need to answer that?) I have purchased the transportable ab-rolling product, because obviously I would gain that six-pack simply by buying the product and using it for three minutes a day, like the model in the infomercial (who, I swear, must be one of those lucky few born with a six-pack). And I must admit, while this one (obviously) did not work, it did provide quite a bit of entertainment during late-night study sessions in my college dorm room, so maybe it was worth the money. I have tried the carb-free diets, the caveman-type diets, the protein-laden diets. I have tried specific vitamins *guaranteed* to speed up one's metabolism. I have tried weight-loss programs that the stars (as well as some normal people) boast of. I've nearly tried it all. To point out the already blatantly obvious, none of these quick-fix solutions did the trick for me. Throughout the bulk of this journey, until just a few years ago, I think there was *maybe* one time that I went for my annual physical and only fell into the overweight category instead of the obese.

OK, let's clarify a few things. First, normally when the doctor checks our weight and determines if we fall into the overweight or obese category, it is based on our BMI (body mass index), which looks at our weight and our height. This can be very misleading, mainly because muscle weighs more than fat. So if your percentage of lean body muscle is great (even if your percentage of body fat is low), you can be classified as overweight. Often, however, this issue with using the BMI is not well explained and people who may be rather fit are told they are overweight or obese. While I am clarifying this for the purposes of this book, I wish this had been the case for me during all those years. But no such luck; I was fat.

One more clarification: I understand that some of these products, diets, and weight-loss programs do work for some people. This is not a blanketed, across-the-board "this product works, this one doesn't." Some people have had huge success, especially with certain weight-loss programs that are *balanced* and actually teach a different way to eat, a different way to understand portion, work in conjunction with exercise, and ultimately introduce a person to a *different way of life*. That's the trick though—the ones that work, that succeed in helping a person not only get healthy but *stay* healthy—offer insight to a lifestyle change. That means not only looking at diet but also looking at physical activity, stress, sleep patterns, emotional health, and (get this) *spiritual health*—a change of life in all dimensions.

* * *

Changing our lives doesn't happen overnight. Yes, changes can happen overnight that will affect everything—a new job offer, a marriage proposal, the unexpected death of a loved one. But taking into our own hands the decision to change our lives—that takes time. It is a process, a journey, that in many ways never ends. It takes dedication, commitment, recommitment, and a drive for something greater—the knowledge that we are both capable of and worth more.

When I train clients, one of the most prominent—and important—aspects of training comes from the conversation of *why*. Why have they decided to spend their time and money on a personal trainer? What has made them decide it's time to get into better physical condition? What do they want out of this experience? What are their short-term goals and aspirations and, complementarily, what are their long-term hopes and dreams? Are they doing this for themselves or for someone else?

Why are you reading this book? What about it caught your eye? What do you hope to gain from this literary experience? What are you hoping for, yearning for, dreaming of? What has your journey been and where do you want it to lead?

* * *

One of the first things I establish with clients is that we will set small goals—realistic, attainable goals. Now, do I believe in dreaming big? Yes. Do I believe in creating change of magnificent magnitude in our world? Yes. Do I think we are capable of becoming new, different, whole persons of faith and hope? Yes. Do I think one person can make a difference, that we can completely change what our lives look like, alter how we see the world, change how we are in the world, assuming we have the resources to do so? Yes, absolutely.

But I have also learned the hard way the need to be realistic, especially when dealing with the change in myself. If I wake up one morning and say, "I'm going to lose forty pounds in five weeks" or, "One month from now I will have a relationship with God that makes me worthy of beatification," I am setting myself up for failure. (Never mind the fact that I would have to change just about everything in my life and being to be compared to Mother

Teresa and somehow acquire major amounts of humility, grace, and holiness; it's never going to happen.)

So we start small: to lose ten pounds in the next eight weeks, to reduce my caloric intake by two hundred calories a day, to exercise five times a week, to cut two cigarettes a day out of my routine, to spend five minutes at the start and end of each day in quiet prayer, to journal more consistently. By setting smaller, more attainable goals, we put ourselves into a place of being able to make these goals actually happen—we are realistic while still setting goals that will take dedication and focus, that aren't necessarily the easiest if we aren't hard at work. Setting goals that are truly attainable makes us feel accomplished when we reach them—and then encourages us to set new goals. It's a process.

What kind of small goals can you set for yourself? What are doable, reasonable changes that you have the power to enact in your life right now, beginning today? To what will you commit yourself, and to what will you continue to choose to commit yourself day after day? Where can you start your process?

* * *

One of the best places to start as we commit to a new path is to figure out what healthy looks like for each of us. Each of us is different and unique—different gifts and talents, weaknesses, and areas of growth.

Let's start with the "healthy on the outside" part of things. The media tells us that "healthy" looks a certain way—that "beautiful" looks a certain way—that in reality is not at all healthy for the majority of the population. Not everyone has a body structure that would be healthy at one hundred five pounds and a size zero or that would support major body-builder biceps and quads. Yet magazines and media continue to tell us that we need to look like the air-brushed women and men we see in magazines. Thank goodness, some movements have begun to combat that idea in recent years, and some magazines (particularly teen magazines geared at girls) are beginning to respond to readers' disgust as the altered images and unrealistic-for-most ideas of what we should look like. It's a beginning, but only a beginning. According to the Renfrew Center Foundation for Eating Disorders, approximately 24 million people in the U.S., of both genders and all ages, suffer from an eating disorder (anorexia, bulimia, and binge eating). That's a huge number. So what do we do—how do we determine what healthy looks like and implement a different way of thinking into our society?

Part of it is feeling comfortable in our own skin. Are you content with how quickly you can run a mile, with how you look in your jeans, with basic movements to walk across the parking lot or carry some boxes up the stairs? Remember, being physically fit does not necessarily mean being skinny. It means we are in good shape and can sustain levels of muscular and cardiovascular strength and endurance and can continue pushing ourselves to maintain some higher levels of physical activity. For some, this will mean wearing a size zero; for others, it will mean a size ten. For some, this will mean benching two hundred fifty pounds; for others, this will mean benching ninety pounds. For some, this might mean walking three miles without stopping; for others, it will be running a marathon.

Each of us has to determine what healthy looks like for us, given our specific body structure and shape, genetics, age, any physical limitations we might have, and so forth. Pushing ourselves to be better, increase our fitness level, achieve more, are all good—as long as we keep ourselves in check mentally, emotionally, and socially. We have to be careful to avoid letting ourselves become so obsessed with working out, exercise, and counting calories that we bring about the exact opposite of what we start the journey wanting; we have to be careful to avoid becoming unhealthy in our search for health.

* * *

"Healthy on the outside" has different manifestations based on who we are, where we come from, and what our history is. It depends on what we are comfortable with and how far we are willing to push ourselves. In many ways, it means defying the status quo set by the media and our surrounding culture. Physical health carries with it a number of varying implications and factors, and the bar is adapted to the stature of the person in many cases.

So what does it look like, then, to be spiritually healthy—"healthy on the inside"? The same principle applies: We are all different, with unique expressions of our faith. The key is having a solid relationship with God, finding ourselves more often in a place of consolation than of desolation. Knowing that when all else around us fails, when we are disappointed in others, in the world, in ourselves, we can turn to God for guidance, for support, for compassion, for strength.

As we grow older, our relationships change. Some friends we have for a lifetime; some are in our lives during certain years for certain reasons; people fall in love, people fall out of love. Our relationships with others are always changing, and we've just finished talking about how our relationship with ourselves can change. As we look at what our goals, hopes, dreams, and aspirations are, we might need to focus ourselves, challenge ourselves, motivate and dedicate ourselves. Similarly, our relationship with God will change as we grow and as we experience the world around us. But keeping God at our core—as our ultimate grandparent, mother, father, brother, sister, friend, confidant (all of the above)—that is where we find ourselves in a spiritually healthy place, when our faith feeds into and informs and shapes all that we do and all that we are.

For some, this may be acquired through attendance at daily Mass; for others, it may come from a weekly volunteer site. Others may find this presence of God most in the community or family to which she belongs; for another, God lies in nature, and a walk around the lake is the place to most be rooted in faith; still others might find this source of spiritual health most through the quiet one-on-one moments with God, when no one else is around and there is pure silence. Just as we are each different and can run a mile in different time frames or can bench different amounts of weight, so too are we different in where we find ourselves most in tune with God's presence.

* * *

So when do we arrive at being healthy? How do we know when it's in our possession, this ever-elusive stage of health? How do we know we've "arrived"? As already noted, it's a journey; there isn't a final destination that, once we get there, we never have to worry about it again. It's not a place we plug into our GPS and we're told exactly how to arrive, and it's not promised to be ours forever once we've got it in our hands. Far from it. Health is constantly being tested and tried and challenged in our lives, on any given day, in any number of ways.

Becoming healthy means looking at each of those six dimensions and figuring out where we are with them. Let's spend a minute working on an activity that I like to do with my first-year students at the start of our Foundations class.

Get out a blank piece of paper and draw a large circle on it. (I'm serious...I want you to actually do this activity right now.) Create six different "pie pieces" by drawing lines from one side of the circle to the other. In each piece, write one of the six dimensions of health: physical, emotional, mental, social, environmental, and spiritual. Use the very center of the circle where all pieces come together as zero. The outer edge of the circle will be considered ten. In each piece—in each dimension—taking into account the definitions and explanations we reflected on in the first chapter, shade in how healthy you are for that specific dimension on a scale of zero to ten. Do this for each dimension of health within the circle (and please, for your own good, be honest. You don't have to share the results with anyone).

Now, take a look at the circle. Are all of the dimensions shaded to the same number? Oftentimes, we are stronger in one area/dimension than in another. We may be at an eight out of ten in the area of our physical health—we work out multiple times a week, eat pretty healthy for the most part, drink socially and safely, and don't smoke. But maybe socially we're only at a five out of ten—we have many acquaintances but not many friends. Most of our conversations, from strangers to family, don't surpass small talk about the weather and the recent accomplishments of our sports teams. We keep to ourselves and hesitate to forge new friendships or take existing friendships to a deeper level. We long for more profound companionship but don't make the time to seek it.

Consider how a wheel turns. It's pretty impossible for a wheel to move smoothly when there are indentations in it, when the circumference is interrupted, when the circle isn't really a circle because it's not perfectly round. (In fact, moving might be impossible, since without being perfectly round, it's not technically a circle.) How, then, can we expect to move smoothly if our health wheel is incomplete, if we don't have a full, functioning circle? We can't move, can we?

So how do we make our wheel turn? Well, it might mean that when we are stronger in some areas than others, we need to scale back a bit in the dimensions on which we've got a pretty good grip. Sometimes to dedicate attention and effort to an area in which we need growth, we have to lessen the efforts we are putting in elsewhere. It's that age-old idea of prioritizing that many of us often struggle with. When I have a stack of papers to grade, a huge student program coming up in two weeks that requires planning, I'm in desperate need of some new moves and choreography in my Zumba® fitness class, and the bathroom is in dire need of a toilet cleaning, the only logical thing to do is try out a new recipe for zucchini bread. My prioritizing skills are *that* extraordinary. But the essence of our being is more crucial than toilet-cleaning, paper-grading, and zucchini bread. Getting our wheel to equal out and roll with ease will dictate everything about our days: our attitude, our energy, how we feel, what we do, who we are, our levels of joy and sadness, whom we help, what we avoid. Our lives depend on our wheel rolling smoothly. It can't *not* be a priority.

So maybe for a while we cut short one of our workouts and spend fifteen minutes of that hour journaling instead of cycling. Maybe we forgo yoga class this week to attend a lecture on global warming being offered at the local university. Maybe we skip happy hour on Thursday to go for a run. Scaling back temporarily in the areas we are secure in—not to the point of detriment, of course—to redirect some energy can be a good thing. I'm going to talk about this a bit more later on, but the idea is to get our wheel in motion. It might mean that two months from now all of our dimensions are at a six instead of some at eight, some at five, one at four, and so forth, but our wheel will be able to turn, to roll, to move. And once we've got our wheel moving along, then over time and with commitment, we can gradually work toward improving in all areas of health and take our wheel from an all-around six to an all-around seven, to an eight...you get the idea.

Checking in on the wheel every few months is a good practice. It allows us to see how we are growing and where attention is needed. It may often correlate with things that are happening in our life and what our surroundings are like in a given time. For example, perhaps the anniversary of a loved one's death is in March. After a few years of following our wheel, we notice that every March when we evaluate ourselves, our emotional and spiritual dimensions reflect lower numbers. Or maybe we notice a pattern that our physical health is at a better place during the summer months. As we notice some of these patterns, it becomes ideal to have some good coping mechanisms and strategies in place for the times when we know one dimension will be a bit lower that enable us to set ourselves up for health despite situations and circumstances outside of our control.

* * *

Part of our human nature is to want to know when we will reach the end, when we will find success, when certain stages of our lives will end and new ones will begin. Likewise, as we move toward health in all of its dimensions, we may be impatient to know when our arrival will be secured, how we will know we are on the right track. This very common aspect of humanity, while perhaps exacerbated by our twenty-first–century instant-gratification tendencies, is not new.

In the Old Testament, five men of the Danite tribe were sent out to explore the land and find a place to settle as they had no inheritance among the tribes of Israel. As they neared Micah's house, they asked the question that, for most of us, time and time again appears on our hearts and in our prayer. "They said to him, 'Consult God, that we may know whether the journey we are making will lead to success'" (Judges 18:5).

How often do we find ourselves wanting the answer to this question—the constant inner inquiry, "Is this worth it?" This struggle appears in life in so many different ways, at different times, for different reasons. A very close friend of mine recently took the bar exam. I recall speaking to him about a month before the exam, and his voice screamed of exhaustion, of weariness, of frustration. He had to be wondering if all the long hours of studying, of burying himself in books, of not seeing friends or family with great frequency, of stress in his relationship because of his schoolwork were going to be worth it. How nice it would be to be assured that indeed it will be worth it, that the journey will be successful, as the Danite men inquired. If we somehow knew ahead of time that we would pass the exam, complete the half marathon, avoid certain illnesses—then we might study, train, and take care of ourselves with more ease and tranquility.

Too bad life doesn't work that way. There's no crystal ball, no road map that God mysteriously places in our crib a few days after we're born, no money-back guarantee on our workouts, our prayer, or the efforts we put forth and the tasks we strive to complete. The response the Danite men received from the priest that day was, "Go in peace! The journey you are making is under the eye of the LORD" (Judges 18:6).

Your journey is favorable. That is, our exploration, our struggles, the chances we take, and the hard work we engage in are good. Sometimes life requires us to ask God for guidance, to listen as closely as we can to what God is nudging us to do (that whole discernment thing the Jesuits are so famous for), to put our nose to the grindstone, to work our tails off, to give 'em a little hell when necessary, and trust that it'll all be OK in the end. Of course, we have to be engaged in journey that is ripe with prayer, care and service for others, and focused on desire.

Desire for what? Thomas Merton, a spiritual author and guru, has left us with much to ponder and reflect on. His profound insights to the spiritual journey based on his experiences, struggles, and uncertainty have been for me a source of great solace and comfort. I particularly love his "The Road Ahead." In this prayer, he speaks to the uncertainty that so many of us—if not all of us at some point in time—experience: uncertainty of self, uncertainty of discerning our call, uncertainty of the road we are on and where our journey and path will lead us. But his words also bring with them, juxtaposed to this sometimes unnerving and unsettling uncertainty, a deep-rooted sense of trust: that because we desire to follow God, and because we source our lives from that desire, the road we walk will be the right road. The path we follow will bring great grace. And we do not walk this road alone, because when we are sourcing ourselves in the desire to know and follow God, we are in constant companionship with our God.

I recall offering this prayer as part of a reflection on my own journey when I was in graduate school. A cherished professor of mine (one of those amazing individuals with whom exists an in-explicable love-hate relationship but who, in the end, teaches you more about yourself in the world than your pride will ever let you admit to his/her face) often joked with me about my "existentialist existence," evident through my love for Merton's words (what he termed, in so many words, as the existentialist prayer). In some ways, he was right. It is a prayer that offers us comfort in knowing that we don't have all (or sometimes it may feel like any!) of the answers, and we follow our hearts as we know they are touched and changed by God and our experience of God in the world. For some, it may sound lofty and intangible. But for those of us who continue to hear, discern, and heed God's call for us on this earth to make God's reign come alive, we have to follow, trusting that God knows what God does. And even if we cannot see where the path is leading, because we trust God—as the Danite men of the Old Testament did—success will come.

The journey has the Lord's approval. The desire to please God does in fact please God. The destination is still TBA and may forever be, but it is the right road to be walking along: the road of faith, health, joy, service, care for all—the road of right relation-ships with God, self, and others, the road of justice. The road may bend, curve, not allow us to see much farther ahead of where we're walking, and bring challenge as well as comfort. But though not always easy, the road is full of peace and love, and if we're lucky, some really good companions to walk with us.

In some ways, the value of the journey has to be enough for us. We don't know what roadblocks we'll hit, how we'll do, if we'll end up meeting our goals. But if we don't try, we'll never know. There's no guarantee on this one, but we must trust and have faith that beginning this journey toward spiritual and physical health—toward the even, calm rotation of our wheel—will lead us to a greater place. It will likely not be perfect, but we've got to make a start. Are you ready?

YOU'RE ALL INVITED

A fairly memorable moment often accompanies a decision to change—or at least accompanies the time we decide we'll try to change. The word *epiphany* comes to mind but has a number of different meanings (including, of course, the celebration of January 6 and the arrival of the Magi). One definition is that of "a sudden, intuitive perception of or insight into the reality or essential meaning of something, usually initiated by some simple, homely, or commonplace occurrence or experience." Something small or some commonplace occurrence for some reason hits us differently, causes us to see the world differently—causes us to see ourselves differently. It's like sitting in Mass one Sunday morning and listening to a gospel reading we've heard a hundred times before, but for some reason on that one Sunday, we're jolted into deep thought and profound reflection on how those words relate to our life, offer perspective on our daily routine, challenge us to think and be different.

In working with clients who are hoping and making efforts to get back in shape, I have found that the desire to change often comes from these little "epiphanies." Maybe it's because they realized for the first time that they are out of breath when they have to climb three flights of stairs, or maybe they struggled picking up a box from the bottom of the closet. Maybe their child is learning to ride a bike without training wheels and they had trouble following behind in case she fell. Or maybe it was sitting on the couch watching television, and for whatever reason, they suddenly realize: *I can't live like this. I am unhealthy, I am unfit, I am unhappy. I need to do something. I need to change.* Whatever the case might be, this "epiphany" can happen at any random moment, any idle Tuesday evening.

Though, perhaps obviously, it doesn't have to happen this way. For others, it may be something big and specific—a doctor tells a woman she really needs to lose weight before trying to get pregnant; an engaged woman knows she will have to be shopping soon for a wedding dress; a young son wants his dad to help him get ready for track-team tryouts—that hurls them into the recognition that they need to dedicate serious time, effort, and attention to their physical health.

Just as I am often contracted for personal training by people who have been led to the decision to invest (time, money, effort) in changing their physical-fitness levels through one of these key moments, I have also encountered many people who have/are going through a spiritual epiphany. Maybe it is sparked by a specific reason—you are asked to be a godparent for a good friend's child; you start attending marriage-preparation classes with your future spouse; a challenging moment arises in life and you feel alone, wondering and questioning where God is in hardship or struggle. Maybe you have recognized yourself in the midst of an existential crisis or are completely clueless about what God is calling you to after graduating from college. Or perhaps it is just a random, unsolicited moment in which someone says something that hits you distinctly, makes you think about your relationship with God, urges you to engage in some introspection about your faith and beliefs. There is no scripted way to experience an epiphany, but you know it when it happens, and once you do, you generally find yourself ready and excited to begin the post-epiphany engagement in discovering a new way of being—renewed in your desire to grow, change, learn, become.

At the risk of being incorrect (which I'm OK with; life is about taking risks, and I'm certainly used to being wrong on occasion),

I am going to assume that if you're reading this book, you may indeed have already had some sort of epiphany of your own. Why else would you spend your time reading and reflecting on this whole idea of health if not because you have come to realize that something in your current way of life might need to change a bit?

What was your epiphany, and when did it happen? Paying attention to the when, where, and how of these moments can be helpful as we grow into a different way of being and as we search for opportunities and encouragement on the journey. Realizing that a change is necessary is the first step—and a huge, important one that cannot go undervalued. But then, of course, comes the "fun" part—figuring out what to do to enact this change and how to make it sustainable.

* * *

One of the biggest pieces of beginning a new stage of the journey is finding others with whom to travel. The whole fact of the matter being that, even when we have no idea where the road is leading, we try to figure it out with others, not alone. We are social beings, and we need other people to grow into the complete persons God calls us to be. What does traveling with another look like? Who do you want walking the road with you? Are you open to companionship? A travel companion on this journey to health will ideally be someone who not only keeps you company but also serves many other purposes: a source of invitation, encouragement, strength, understanding, compassion, hope, accountability, challenge; someone who will push you to do more, be more, give more, love more, work more, grow more.

A companion on our physical-health journey may be a friend who will come to the gym with us, take a yoga class with us, or join us for a game of pickup basketball on a Friday afternoon. It might be a spouse or partner who commits to training for a marathon with us so we don't have to run alone. It might be a personal trainer we hire to coach us through workouts and push us to constantly increase our strength and endurance and to guide us in ways to improve our physical fitness. It may be people we meet in a fitness class or boot camp who, after seeing those same regulars every Monday, Wednesday, and Friday at 5:30 AM, become our support, our community, our accountability partners. When we find a group of people with the same drive and determination, we grow to count on those people—and when one person is missing, the absence is felt and the atmosphere changes.

How do we intentionally find this person, these people? If it's not someone who is already built into our social network (family, friends, coworkers), we may have to put ourselves on the line a bit. Be vocal and open about your desire to get back in shape, to find a workout routine you like and can stick with, to ask around and see if people know a good personal trainer, to try out a few different fitness classes at a few different studios or gyms to see which one fits you best.

For quite some time I taught a late-night Zumba class. It started around 8:15 and, generally speaking, attracted the same group of regulars. Sure, we'd have new people here and there, but for the most part, the same core group religiously showed up at our dance studio on Monday and Wednesday evenings at 8:15. It really became more than "just" a Zumba class. It became a place where people could let go, forget about the week's stressors and struggles and hardships, put their responsibilities out of their mind for an hour and lose themselves in the music, in the sweat, in the workout.

A person, however, could find all of those things at just about any Zumba class—staple components of the Zumba fitness phenomenon. Our class was more than that; our class became a community. People hugged one another when they came through the door before class. They exchanged recipes for new, healthy dinner options they had tried and liked. They noticed if one person was missing and made sure to contact that person and check in with him/her. They laughed, had fun, enjoyed not just the class but one another's company (and once in a while complained together too, but only on the days when the workout really took a toll on them). It really was quite the community.

* * *

So where do we find this (albeit perhaps metaphoric) Zumba class full of really cool people to take this journey with us? All it takes is just one person to extend a personal invitation, and the shared journey can start right then and there. When I moved to the city in which I now reside, I knew one person. I didn't know her well; we were acquaintances who had networked with some mutual people. But she knew I was new to the area, and I remember her saying to me, "I am just going to invite you to everything. You can come or not come, I don't mind either way, but until you tell me to stop, I am just going to invite you along to everything." It was the absolute best thing she could have done for me, and I was so grateful for her kind and hospitable approach. It has very much colored the way I now welcome people into the city, community, and school where I work—with a much deeper sense of invitation. By her inviting me (to Zumba class, salsa dancing, going out to eat with healthier options), she really had a major influence on what I chose to do and how, after that, I chose to direct my energy and personal efforts.

That invitation is what really sparked my commitment to improve my physical health. One person's giving me the example and offering to connect me to the Zumba fitness program, and from there, I ran with it and never looked back (other than to appreciate where I had come from). By joining the Zumba bandwagon, I got hooked...due, of course, to the fun, the music, and the adrenaline rush of the workout, but due also to the people I met and the friends I made through going to the same Zumba class a few times a week.

My life literally did a one-eighty due to one person's going out of her way to extend a broad invite.

* * *

We all have different personalities and play different roles in communities. Are you the one in your group who is always setting the day, time, and place for your friends' gatherings? If so, then maybe the change comes from what you decide you and your girlfriends will do on a Friday night. Maybe you all take a yoga class and then go for smoothies instead of out for drinks one night. Make the shift if that's your role. Maybe it means expressing to your spouse an interest in trying something physically demanding, and then she does some research on what you could do together, or having an honest conversation with a lifelong friend about your desire to get in shape and asking her to help you find the courage to get a trial membership at the gym. Making the decision to adjust your physical-activity levels doesn't require you to completely transform your personality, but it does require you to push a little further and challenge your comfort zone a bit. Don't be afraid to offer an invitation—and don't be afraid to accept one either.

* * *

This same method can be applied to our spiritual health as well. All it takes is that invitation. Maybe it's asking a friend to join you for Mass one Sunday. Maybe it's inviting an acquaintance to join you for a night of ecumenical praise and worship. Maybe it's going to hear a speaker at the local university who is speaking about faith and politics and striking up a conversation about the presentation with the person sitting next to you after it ends. Maybe it's joining a group in your area that focuses on faith-based discussions. Perhaps you search out the local chapter of JustFaith or a community-service opportunity at your local parish.

Like a companion on the physical-health journey, someone who accompanies us on our spiritual journey must be willing to walk with, support, and encourage us—and also challenge us and push us to be more, love more, trust and believe more, question more, reflect more, understand more. The Jesuits have a phrase they often use for this: striving for *the magis*—that is, literally translated, "more." Searching for more in our faith journey doesn't always mean quantitatively. In fact, much more often our spiritual "more" is focused on the qualitative. It is challenge rooted in love.

Who can both accompany and challenge you spiritually? Part of this question might first be addressed by figuring out where/how your spiritual needs are fed. Does your spirit feel nourished through liturgy, maybe attending Mass at the same church and listening to the same preacher each week? Or do you find yourself thriving more through informal prayer with others or perhaps living in an intentional Christian community? Maybe you feel most close to God when you are engaged in faith-based service and reflection. Or perhaps being with others from another culture whose lives speak to their faith in a form different from what you have known and that offers you an opportunity for self-reflection and thought is what most poignantly sparks your spiritual growth and development. Maybe it's all of the above, maybe it's none of the above. What makes you, and when do you feel, spiritually alive?

Who accompanies us once we understand more about who we are and the situations that best feed our souls and faith? Many people who are focused on their spiritual growth and development may enlist the companionship of a spiritual director. A spiritual director can be a remarkably important companion on the journey toward spiritual health. He/she can often listen with an unbiased, somewhat removed perspective that allows for insight unhindered by a personal disposition. Oftentimes spiritual directors are trained to listen to a person and to help us bring our faith to a different, deeper place through reflective questions, feedback, and challenge us to more fully understand what God is communicating to us through life experiences and situations.

Teachers can also be amazing people to walk with on our journey toward a place of greater spiritual health. Probably most common are teachers we find in a college or graduate class—those who have lived and discovered their faith in the intellectual context, spending hours poring over Scripture, the works of long-ago spiritual writers (such as the Desert Fathers), and the current commentaries and thoughts on what our faith means as we move and relate and react to the signs of the times. Take the time to even just audit a theology class at your local Catholic university and you're likely to be presented with new ways of thinking and believing that can spark a new direction as you walk along this road called faith. Teachers, then, can be pivotal guides as we move into new phases of questioning, understanding, and believing. Forming relationships with those teachers gives us opportunities for more personal insight through conversation and dialogue that can throw us into all sorts of new realms of reflection.

* * *

Or perhaps those spiritual companions come in the most unanticipated of experiences. About once a month I have breakfast with a small group of about six older gentlemen (sometimes one other female joins us as well). These men come from an amazing variety of experiences. Some were missionaries in Latin America for nearly two decades, and some spent a number of years in their earlier lives as priests. Not all are Catholic but represent other denominations of Christianity. A few are activists of some sort whose passion is rooted in Catholic social teaching and a faith that works for and lives justice. Most teach (or have taught) at the university level—in theology, international relations, political science, and so forth. They have invited me into their breakfast club—though I am young enough to be their granddaughter, have not experienced firsthand the changes that the Second Vatican Council brought to the world, cannot come anywhere near being on a par with their life experiences, cannot offer remotely close to what they bring to the table in intellectual stimuli, and carry nowhere near the understanding of the Church in the modern world that they do.

These men, who often remind me of my grandfather in their love of coffee, conversation, and devotion to God and the Blessed Mother, serve as amazing companions for me on the spiritual journey. Every time I'm with them, I leave our shared meal that morning thinking (a) I should really return to school; (b) I need to order a subscription to the *New York Times* and *America* magazine; and (c) how incredibly lucky I am to belong to a church that includes people such as these gentlemen. They are fellow wayfarers on the road who show me what it is to both challenge and love the family unit of which we are a part, how to be of a world I know and believe in and want to be better than, and who remind me not to get discouraged at the grand tasks ahead in making that hope a reality. They continue to be examples of a constant ebb-and-flow sense of living that strives for wholeness, knowing that our flawed humanity will likely always preclude us from achieving that fullness. They remind me, in the most subtle of ways on Wednesday mornings over breakfast tacos and a bit of salsa verde, that spiritual health is a prime example of our faith's "already/not yet"—that in some ways where we already are and what we do is God's kingdom alive all around and among us, and yet we must constantly strive to bring about God's kingdom and create Scripture's vision of community on earth. They also remind me that in my struggles to understand God, creation, community, and my role in this world, I am in very good company.

* * *

Sometimes the best discussions about spirituality and faith and life come from something we hear in the homily at Mass—you know, that moment where something the priest says hits you so strongly that you repeat it over and over in your head while you search in your purse for a pen to jot any little amount of it down on the really thin edges of the bulletin so you can go back to it later. But the key to understanding what goes on at church and in our world and faith tradition is talking about it—more so, *living it*—with other people. Our Catholic faith invites us—and more so, calls us—to community. We live a faith that not only tells us to work for justice if we want peace (thank you, Paul VI!) but to be part of a community that engages in ritual and tradition together, where we know that no matter what church building we walk into in whatever part of the country, we will find the same words, prayers, and order of events that make us feel at home. The sense of knowing what's coming next—even if just for an hour and even if in a building where we don't know anyone else's name—gives us a sense of grounding, safety, and familiarity that often only accompanies family.

Those spiritual experiences and life-giving discussions about faith can also come from completely unrelated, unique, and unexpected events. I have spent years over the past decade living in and out of community. One of my most prominent experiences of living in community occurred when I spent time in South America as a missionary with a long-term Catholic volunteer program. I lived with other young adults as we learned a new language, took on jobs for which we were completely unskilled and unprepared, dealt with sickness and confusion and difficulty, and attempted to be with and offer compassion to those with whom we lived and worked. Those who over time became our Ecuadorian family and friends taught us amazing lessons about life, love, faith, humility, suffering, and God that would forever change our way of being, the decisions we would make, and the ways in which we enter into relationship with others.

The two years I spent living on the equator were two of the most beautiful, tear-ridden, challenging, heart-breaking, joy-filled, and overwhelmingly altering years that I have ever lived through to date and dare guess I may ever live and grow through again. The experiences with which I was gifted and the people with whom I shared those years left indelible marks on the formation of my faith and taught me—more than I could have ever anticipated—what consolation and desolation truly are.

Those with whom I have been in community over the years have often become for me some of the clearest, most constant sources of spiritual companionship. During my experiences of living in community, those with whom I have shared life, meals, prayer, service, joys, and sadness have helped to guide me on my journey, always striving toward greater awareness, health, happiness, wholeness, and consolation. They challenged me, asked hard questions, comforted me, annoyed me (and let me annoy them), supported me, and loved me. They very much, day in and day out, demonstrated to me what the Incarnation is all about and offered a radical hospitality—a window into growth of my own heart and soul through faith.

* * *

Companions on the journey are a vital component to our physical and spiritual health. Without others to offer us insight and perspective, challenge and support, share our joy and pain, we'll never make it. Not only will we suffer from great loneliness, but we will (almost assuredly) not find the strength to better ourselves and our world without the presence of community.

Who is your companion on your journey toward spiritual health? Who challenges you to be more and do more and live more fully? Whom do you let onto the road with you to share stories, hardships, discernment, the search for passion, and to bear the load of a cross that demands we strive for peace and justice in our oftentimes very difficult world?

Has anyone ever offered you this type of hospitality? An invitation to journey, an invitation to join, an open invitation to discover new parts of yourself, your inner joy, your passions, new adventures, new challenges, new hopes and dreams and approaches to the world? Have you ever offered this type of radical hospitality? It's not the "let's go out to lunch and talk about the weather and our children's teachers" type of hospitality. It's a reaching out, an openness, a metaphoric (or sometimes tangible) embrace; it's a vulnerability that allows others in, knowing they might change us, and being willing to take on the responsibility that we might change them as well. It's a desire to share and love and care deeply for another physically and spiritually—emotionally, socially, mentally, environmentally—to care not only for who they are but for who they can become and who we can become by walking with them.

* * *

This tug to be better and do more is a feeling many of us will experience in life. Though we may at times along the journey find ourselves content and happy with our health, more often than not we will find ourselves thinking, *I could be better. I could run faster, live more, eat better; I could pray more, treat others more kindly, be a more faithful servant.* This is natural, but it's necessary to take a look at what motivates our desire to constantly strive for more. Do we aim for more as a means of constantly striving for better, more right relationships with God, ourselves, and others? Well, ideally of course, that would be the reason behind exercising more, studying more, discovering more about ourselves and what makes us "tick," reading more, volunteering more, praying more—you get the idea. Ultimately we hope that all we do and are, with an emphasis on improving in all of the dimensions of health, lead to greater relationships—lead to greater justice.

Sometimes however, when we are honest with ourselves, that desire to do more and be more can develop from a not-as-healthy place within us. Rather than the push for greater health coming from a desire to be more in tune with God, ourselves, and the world, it can come from a place of constant self-doubt and/or unceasing self-criticism. We exercise more and eat less because our ex-boyfriend is dating a girl who is skinnier. We choose a more difficult major in college because of a need to win out in sibling rivalry. We push ourselves mentally to gain more letters after our name because it will bring status and money rather than letting it be a true passion and vocation. We (OK, not me, because we all know that gender is going to inhibit this one, but for you males out there) enter the seminary because grandma always wanted a priest in the family and you were the logical choice. We study certain tracks and play certain sports and marry certain people because that's what society says to do, that's what is expected of us, that's what is "normal." And if we don't look a certain way or have a certain degree, we have to go back and try to "fix" it—because if we only get into that dress or earn that PhD, we can stop being so self-deprecating, we can finally be seen as successful, we can be happy.

These are the wrong reasons for changing, for striving for the *magis*; they are unhealthy reasons for wanting greater physical and spiritual health. The move to change must come from within, for the greater good of self, others, and God—not as a response to societal pressures or familial expectations. Our health is based very much on our heart. Yes, on the functioning of this key muscle in our body and also on its stirrings, on its desires, and how we let our heart know God and others and work to know both more.

The heart must be the source of our days, of our movements, of our successes and struggles, of our striving for justice.

* * *

I was training a woman once who had almost no experience working out—as in ever. She came to my Zumba classes once in a while, and when the studio offered a small-group personal-training weight-loss challenge, she signed on. On the outside, she had it all together. She was a successful doctor, had beautiful children, was obviously bright and capable of so much, and seemed happy enough. As I began training her and she sparingly offered bits and pieces about her life, it became clear that her participation in this new group exercise wasn't about the outside; it wasn't (just) about wanting to lose weight and get into shape. It was so much deeper than that. It was about her relationship with herself—wanting to gain confidence and assuredness and feel good about who she was. It was about her relationship with others—her desire to set an example for her children of self-care and commitment and how to see something deeper than what is on the outside, the shallow image that the world sees when they look at a person. It was about understanding herself and her role in the world more concretely, her wanting to be healthy and happy in all of its various and multiple dimensions. Her choice to "get healthy" was about so much more than losing weight; it was about finding herself and understanding more fully the person God had created her to be.

* * *

When I start training people, I often find that what starts as their wanting me to tell them how many push-ups to do, what key foods to avoid eating, and their desire to drop a few pounds really becomes so much more than that. What they end up wanting from me—whether they like to admit it or not—is someone outside their circle to listen. They are looking for a safe space to vent, talk, cry, take out frustration; in other words, an unbiased sounding board. I often find myself more than slightly grateful for that minor I picked up in counseling during my undergraduate career and wondering if this is the type of "therapy" I used to hear talked about when women went to get their hair done decades ago. (You know, that stereotype that women tell all the juicy and dramatic details about their lives to their hairdressers. Maybe it's true.)

I'm OK with taking on a different role from that of someone who shows a client how to execute a certain exercise to get a certain result. In reality, if you're working out on the anniversary of a loved one's death or in the midst of a crisis at work or struggling in a relationship—it's *going* to affect how much energy you have, and you are going to need/want to talk about it. So if I can offer a place where someone can work and grow through something, whether it be a weight-loss plateau, a desire for more muscular strength, improving cardiovascular endurance, or a need to have someone witness their pain or joy or struggle...it's all part of the bigger picture. One piece of our hearts, souls, bodies, and being affecting another—paying attention to all those aspects is what I can focus on with my clients one person, one journey at a time. It is a gift to be a companion for others on their journey. It is a gift to be in relationship with those striving for more right relationships all around.

* * *

The crux of the how, why, when, and who (we are becoming) of the journey of health is twofold: one, the reason(s) behind our desire to improve when we enter new phases of the journey—when we exercise more, work out harder, pray more fervently, engage in more meaningful conversations, listen more intently, think more deeply, and work toward living more fully; two, whom we walk the journey with. We may take the plunge for reasons we never disclose or for reasons we might not even fully be aware of, but rarely—and I would argue never—does it really just boil down to one solitary reason. Undoubtedly, one single result is not what we will get from a new focus and approach to health.

Just as undoubtedly, we cannot walk that road alone. There was a method behind the madness of Jesus' sending his disciples out in pairs and groups. We are built for discovering, journeying, and growing together in community. Whether it is to share in our prayer, spot us on a weight lift, tell us to think twice before we eat that ice cream, or give us a hug on the day we think there is no possible way we could understand the world and God's movements less, we need one another.

* * *

Why do you want to change? Why do you want to be better, be healthier, in any and all of the dimensions? What's behind your heart's desire to be healthy? Are you shifting and changing and growing and challenging for the right reasons? Who is with you? Who is in your corner, and who walks this journey with you? To whom do you offer hospitality, support, and a share in the stirrings of your heart? Who holds you accountable, who keeps you honest? Whose life are you changing through invitations you make? Who keeps you going to class and brings you recipes for healthy dinners; with whom do you eat tacos and talk about changing the world?

My life changed drastically with one person's extending an invite. So I ask, who has invited you…to change physically, emotionally, mentally, environmentally, socially, spiritually? To whom have you extended an invitation? And, ultimately, to that which God is inviting all of us on a daily basis: to knowing God greater and more deeply, to care for others more profoundly, to grow as persons of faith and love. Are you ready to accept the invitation?

IT'S A BOTH/AND

In my work in ministry—which is a daily invitation to walk with young adults on their spiritual journey, accompanying them toward a greater understanding of God, self, and others—I often ask students to reflect on and discern their passion. Similarly, when I start working one on one with new clients in personal training, we first have a conversation about what they enjoy doing, what motivates them to get up and moving, and what kinds of activities bring them happiness. In both cases, we are trying (literally) to get to the heart of the matter: What is your passion?

How do we define passion? Where does it come from? How do we get it? How do we fuel it? How do we share it? How do we encourage others to find their own passion—to explore, discover, question, wonder, wander, create, thrive in, strive for, and give themselves to that passion? For that matter, how do we personally do all of those things in relation to our own passion? And where does living our passion lead us?

A passion is something we love to do. Maybe we have a passion for dance or music; maybe we have a passion for running or swimming; perhaps our passion is in reading and writing or maybe being presented with a ridiculously complex equation and having to spend hours pooling together the various lessons we've learned in math class over the years to finally come up with an answer. I have often heard people say they have a passion for helping people. Most of my friends (though, sadly, not all) who are educators would say they have a passion for teaching. Some might have a passion for coaching or understanding the biomechanics of the body (how and why it works the way it does) or perhaps exercise physiology (how our body changes and adapts to the different exercises we do and the physical conditions we put the body through). Any of these things—and much, much more—can be a passion. Very simply, a passion is what we love. However, when it comes to developing our passions, a lot more comes into play than simply "I really love to do this."

I love to sing. Ever since I was little, as quite the extroverted child who demanded insane amounts of attention and had to be around people all the time (I have become much more introverted over the years, thankfully), I would sing constantly. I sang along with the Disney movies I watched and along with the tapes my mom would play in the car on long rides to family gatherings. I sang along with the radio, I sang along with my best friend as we played Care Bear records on our Cinderella record player. (I fear half the people reading this book will have no idea who the Care Bears are, much less have ever even seen a record player.) I could say that earlier in life I had a passion for singing.

Now, here's the thing: I am absolutely, 100 percent, unquestionably, painfully tone deaf. My sister once told me that she refuses to sit next to me in church because I throw her off so terribly when I sing. (When I threw back the whole "Singing is like praying twice!" theory, she rolled her eyes and assured me that God would much rather listen to my prayers in the words of a whisper than to cringe through my rendition of the "Servant Song.") No matter how much I wish I could carry a tune, I came to realize, much to my disappointment, that there is absolutely no hope for me.

Most often, what we love to do has to be coupled with at least *some* ability to execute that passion. Now, I'm not saying we need to be amazing at what we love to do. We don't even necessarily need to be all that incredibly good at it. But at the very least, I would hope that what you love to do wouldn't send people running in the other direction at Olympic speeds. Oftentimes, part of why we love to do what we do is because we're moderately decent at it. As we learn to develop a passion, it is not only about doing what we love but about how we grow in that passion, become better at it, use it for the greater good, use it to serve others. Ideally, one's passion—over time and experience and growth and striving to improve in that passion—would lead to a more clear way in which to respond to the needs of the world around us and create a more just, fair, and peaceful community. Ideally, our passion leads to our vocation.

Passion, at its best, would be healthy. I trust you are not going to find yourself passionate about smoking, eating junk food, engaging in drug activity, or sitting in front of the television or computer for hours on end. Sure, you might have a passion for food, television, and computers; but how can you use those things, learn more about them, discover more about yourself in relation to them in a way that is healthy and beneficial for the greater good? Maybe a passion for food drives you to study to be a dietician or nutritionist. Maybe a love for computers leads you to website design for nonprofits. Perhaps an interest in television leads you to study the effects of media on teenagers' self-confidence or how television can be used for creating awareness about social issues of our time.

We hope that our individual passion will be based in goodness, that it will manifest itself in a healthy way that will allow us to bring that goodness into the world in unique and special forms through our lives and vocations. Ideally, our passion allows us to be in the world in a more complete and whole way, sourcing ourselves from goodness, love, and our call to serve God and the world.

* * *

I would be remiss not to address one very critical piece in this challenge to search for our passions, our health, our freedom. Passion does indeed speak to our desires, hopes, loves, and that about which we feel strongly; we have no choice but to focus our lives around these loves. But passion—particularly in our Catholic faith—also speaks to suffering, as in the passion of Christ when he suffered and died on the cross. Like many words in our language, *passion* has more than one meaning. How is this relevant, and how are the meanings connected?

It's not always easy to figure out what we are passionate about and how to live that passion. It often takes time and lots of effort, some trial and error, and some decent life experience to figure out what is truly our passion. We might discover we have a passion for something we never dreamed we'd even have remote interest in, much less a desire to focus our life around. And while passions are sources of life and energy and desire, they also demand hard work.

Although it is important for us to find out what we love, it is just as important to figure out what we *don't* love. At times, the "trial and error" approach is the most effective—giving ourselves an opportunity to try something we think we may or may not enjoy, be good at, find joy in, and being OK with the outcome. This can be difficult, especially if we have been raised in a "failure is not an option" way of thinking. Although discovering that which is *not* our passion is certainly not a failure, it may seem that way to us if we are not open to its place in our journey. We must open ourselves to the bigger picture, the wider search, if we are to accept that which we come to understand is not our passion as a way of moving toward that which is.

Discovering that which is not our passion can be painful at times. I know for a fact that I do not love being in administrative roles. I have taken on such roles in my professional life (some by choice, some not) enough to have figured out (the hard way, one might say) that it is not my passion. While those experiences brought with them some hardship and suffering, it was only by being in those roles that I was able to figure out what my passion was not and therefore continue to discover my true passions and pursue them wholeheartedly. It took some suffering to find what I love.

Anyone who has ever lost weight can verify that it's hard work. It requires dedication and commitment, focus on diet and exercise. But for those of us who have been through a significant weight-loss journey, it also very much becomes a passion: a love for the journey to health, the journey to fitness, the journey toward wellness. As the old adage goes, "If it were easy, everyone would do it." Finding our passion is not easy and will oftentimes bring suffering and sacrifice with it during the journey. But the reward is great.

I'm sure you know people who are in a job they don't necessarily like. They go to work, clock in, fulfill their responsibilities of the shift, clock out, and go home. Their job does not give them a sense of purpose or fulfillment, a sense of joy or energy—it's a paycheck. Now, although I don't advocate a "live to work" approach to our days, I do advocate filling our lives with what we enjoy, that simultaneously makes us a better person and this world a better place. That's the whole idea of vocation, after all—finding/creating/engaging in that which allows our heart's desires to respond to the needs of the world.

Sometimes we try things we think might be it and discover they aren't. That's OK. Again, it's part of the bigger picture and wider search for our passion. At other times, we may try something and we think, *Well, this doesn't seem like I'm going to love it, but I'll give it a try and see what happens.* This small step might lead us to the discovery of a passion, finding something we never even imagined we would love. These passions lead us to new experiences, new places, new opportunities, and new ways of being in the world.

I believe physical and spiritual health are manifestations of inner passions. Meaning that I think when we figure out what we love—both by way of our physical being and by way of our spiritual being—we'll find ourselves healthy. We'll look at this a little more tangibly in the next chapter, but try to grasp the beginning of this idea now: When we find something we physically love to do—running, dancing, swimming, cycling, yoga—we want to engage in this activity, we want to do it often, we want to get better at it, and then ultimately we find ourselves in a place of greater physical health. Similarly, when we find something we love spiritually—quiet prayer time, going to Mass, sharing conversation about faith and the world with friends, trusting a greater Being when we have a hard time trusting ourselves—these are ways in which we can develop and grow more fully in our spiritual health and wholeness.

* * *

I believe, very much, that God wants us to be healthy—to be secure in each dimension of health and feel confident, capable, and competent—and to recognize how precious our bodies and our health are. In Saint Paul's First Letter to the Corinthians, we read, "Do you not know that your body is a temple of the holy Spirit within you, whom you have from God, and that you are not your own? For you have been purchased at a price. Therefore, glorify God in your body" (6:19–20).

It might sound corny to some, but it's true—our bodies are temples. It took me a long time to realize just how true—and just how much of a responsibility—that is. Jesus was born of the Blessed Virgin Mary and became human. He took on a human body, complete with aches and pains, the choice to respect his body or not, to care for his body or not, to take his body and the ability to move and exercise for granted or not. As Christians who strive to live in the example of Christ and to follow the path he laid for us, we must face the choice to respect our bodies (or not), care for our bodies (or not), take our ability to move and exercise for granted (or not). We often talk about seeing the face of Christ in others and reflecting the face of Christ for others. If that is truly part of our calling as Christians, as Catholics—then we must make the decision to honor and respect and care for our bodies, as they are vessels of the Incarnation, vessels of Christ Jesus. Our bodies are sacred and holy and deserve the care and attention that come with being focused on our physical health.

How do you see your body as a vessel of the Incarnation? What are the ways in which you honor yourself as a manifestation of Christ, as a temple of the sacred, as a carrier of the Holy Spirit? Do you recognize the divine within you?

Think about what you would do if you met Jesus today. How would you welcome him? How would you care for him? Would you offer him whatever was in the cabinet or would you take care to prepare him a full, balanced, delicious meal that would nourish his body and give him strength to go out into the world—full of vitamins, nutrients, good grains, substantial food and crisp water for hydration so that, even on the hottest of days, he would have the stamina and sustenance to carry out his mission, walking with people, preaching to people, being an example for people of how to live well? If Jesus were to be your house guest, would you want him to be occupied all night, out late drinking heavily, not resting, not taking the time to listen to his body's needs before preparing for his next leg of the journey? Or would you offer him a comfortable bed and restful space to rejuvenate?

Do you do that for yourself? Do you offer yourself hospitality and welcome? Do you care for your body through balanced meals, nourishment, sufficient sleep? Are you gentle with yourself, giving yourself time and space to be social with friends, to sleep an adequate amount, to fill your body with the nutrients it needs, to stay hydrated and well fed? Why would you treat Jesus so different than you might treat yourself, knowing that you are indeed called to be a speaker of the Word, your body, a home for Christ?

* * *

As we look at how we would receive Christ, how we would care for Christ's health, and subsequently how we care for ourselves and strive to pay smart attention to our own health, I think it is also important that we recognize how we view health in the context of the larger world and the issues that face our global community. Christ is not just present in your being or mine but in the being of all humanity—all of our sisters and brothers around the world. How is each person, each carrier of Christ, being cared for and having their needs attended to in a healthy and all-encompassing way?

When we aren't eating well (failing to eat balanced, nutritious meals and consuming only enough food to sustain us but not over-indulge), we are taking both our bodies and our resources for granted. According to the *Oxford English Dictionary,* hunger is defined as "the want or scarcity of food in a country." World hunger, then, aggregates that to a global level; the related technical term is malnutrition. Malnutrition means a lack of nutrients, vitamins, and minerals that are necessary for human health.

Despite the fact that one in seven people in the world suffer from hunger (World Hunger Education Service), our global agriculture actually produces enough to satisfy every person with approximately 2,720 calories per person per day. Many of us in the First World concern ourselves with how many calories we consume daily—making sure we don't consume too many so as to gain weight, spend more money on low-calorie food items, purchase severely overpriced organic, fat-free, low-calorie juices and smoothies. (Check out some of the natural juice cleanses. They can run up to $80 a day if you want to buy their product to get into those skinny jeans for a big night out.) On the other end of the spectrum, we in the First World oftentimes consume many more calories than we need; we eat until we are full, not until we are no longer hungry. We go to a dinner party and the host is sure to have a wide variety of foods, something for everyone. We try it all, even though we might not be feeling hunger anymore after finishing our first plate because it "just looks so good!"

We all fall into that trap. But let's remember that while we are trying either to limit our caloric intake to unhealthy amounts or enjoying much more food than our bodies need, one in three children in developing countries are suffering from malnutrition. I have a hard time comprehending this reality, given the resources available in our world today. There is a deep connection between the way in which we care for our own selves and how we care for the health of the world at large. How do our decisions affect the lives of others? How do we strive for justice—health—for all? As we look at our global community, how does our consumption and the way in which we attend to our physical state of health relate to the opportunities for healthy living that exist in other parts of the world?

How can we possibly take our physical health for granted? How can we take for granted the foods that surround us and consume so many more calories than we need? Recalling our conversation about environmental health, how can we take for granted our ability to walk outside, exercise, work out, enjoy fitness classes? Recognizing how many people in the world do not have access to such things, how can we not make use of all that we have at our disposal to help guide us in a physically healthy lifestyle? How can we not appreciate the luxury of having such things available to us? And more so, how can we not fight for these opportunities—sufficient caloric intake, access to clean water, safe spaces to play and exercise? How can we refrain from the fight to make these available to all people in all places? Isn't it only fair that all people should have the opportunity to live a healthy life should they so choose?

* * *

It is my firm belief that God wants us to couple our health with happiness. God wants us to be happy. But more than that, God desires for us this combination of health and happiness—which is also known as *wellness.* As we think about this journey toward our own physical and spiritual health and the ways in which our state of being (healthy) affects the world around us, let us return then to that which brings us this combination of health and happiness: our passions.

Think for a few minutes about your physical-health and personal-exercise journey. What kind of activities do you enjoy? What's your favorite way to work out? Do you prefer exercising with a group, like in a fitness class or group-training setting, or do you like being on your own, sweating and struggling and feeling successful on your own time and in your own space? Do you have the motivation to work out alone or do you need others to get you going? Do you need music to set your pace or do you like being outside, listening to the sounds of the world around you? What keeps you going when you want to quit? Is it your own stubbornness, your willpower, your competitive nature, your fear of failure? Or is it the friend next to you saying, "Come on, just fifteen more minutes," a reassuring and encouraging smile from your fitness-class instructor, your trainer telling you that you're already halfway through the set, or Pitbull's lyrics talking about going from eviction and food stamps to "Mr. Worldwide" set to an upbeat tempo?

Once you figure out what you love to do, it can expand into a whole world of opportunities, bringing you new life and energy. Exercise—and the scary and overwhelming connotation that word often brings with it—becomes much more conquerable and, in my experience, way more enjoyable. Suddenly, a love and passion for music has turned into a regular exercise routine that brings you amazing heart-healthy benefits.

Sometimes, however, it takes a while to figure out what we love and how to go about engaging in that in such a way that results in a solid progression in our physical health. Some students come to my Zumba class, ready to give up after trying class after class and not finding an instructor who fits their style. Every instructor is totally different, and so every class has a different feel. If you like hip-hop, you go to one instructor. If you enjoy dancing and moving your hips, you go to another. If you want more of a fitness-aerobic feel to the Latin rhythms, you might end up in my class. In the Zumba program at least, the trick is *finding what you like*, taking it, and running with it. Let it become a way of life for you.

Why would you let a form of exercise become a way of life? Why would you allow some specific fitness activity to become a priority? Well, other than the obvious reasons of weight management, disease prevention, heart health, and so forth, there's the opportunity for building community and making friends. It's amazing how many people I have met through the fitness industry. But even beyond all that, there is still a greater reason to let physical fitness become not just something we do in our spare time but a way of life: ultimately, it leads one to God.

* * *

Martha Graham was a dancer and choreographer from Pennsylvania. She spent her life dedicated to dance, to sharing her spirit through her unique and creative movements, to influencing the world of dance in extraordinary measures. She is quoted as having said, "I am a dancer. I believe that we learn by practice. Whether it means to learn to dance by practicing dancing or to learn to live by practicing living….In each, it is the performance of a dedicated, precise set of acts, physical or intellectual, from which comes shape of achievement, a sense of one's being, a satisfaction of spirit. One becomes in some area an athlete of God."

I think Martha was on to something, though I would argue that it is not a set of acts that might be physical or intellectual that leads to a sense of one's being, but rather it is a both/and. Just as passion is a both/and: It is both what we love and it is suffering that ultimately leads to health and freedom. Similarly, by living a dedication to both physical movement and intellectual efforts, we become who we are called to be, we grow more fully into the creation God offers the world in our individual presence. So how do we dedicate ourselves to these components of our being?

Some might say we need to fully achieve health in one dimension (physical, mental, emotional, environmental, social, spiritual) before we can fully move on to another. I believe there is a lot of validity here, though it is important to remember that health—in all its dimensions—is a journey more than a destination, meaning we are constantly needing to focus attention without letting things slip, even after achieving a good, solid place of health in a specific dimension. I am a firm believer that as we focus on and succeed in one dimension or area, when we get to a solid foundation, we have the freedom to move into another dimension more—give more of ourselves to the new dimension we take on. By having the courage to discover one's passion in one realm of health, over time and growth and assurance of that passion (achieving that place of dimension-specific health), you grow into a place of freedom to discover your passion in the other realm.

It takes courage to make this leap. Making oneself vulnerable, admitting that we are not fully healthy, not fully the people God is calling us to be, that we have room for growth and are willing to put ourselves on the line to change—that takes guts. It takes a person who is OK with recognizing that "I'm not perfect. I could be better than I am right now. And not only could I be better, but I am willing to work hard and put forth effort to get there. I'm willing to invest myself—my heart, time, money, and great effort—to get to a better place." It isn't easy. It isn't easy to try new things and not know where they'll lead, to risk failure and disappointment as part of the journey to something greater than what and where we are now. Finding and growing in passion and embarking on this lifelong journey of good health, of wellness, is certainly not for the faint-hearted.

Are you willing? Are you willing to change and be changed? Are you willing to commit yourself, to dedicate yourself, to invest in that which you might still not fully envision? You don't necessarily know what it looks like. Are you willing to take the first step into the unknown? Remember Merton's words—you do not (necessarily) know where you are going. Do you trust in God and in your own desire to get there? Are you willing to put yourself on the line to get healthy? It might mean giving up or cutting back on some things you enjoy (like bread or ice cream). It might mean going through struggle and some suffering to find yourself in a place of great love and joy. Are you willing to open yourself up, to allow yourself to burst forth into passion, into freedom, into health?

If we are willing, if we are courageous, so much awaits us. Indeed, this passion (finding what we love to do and diving into it full force) leads to health. The etymology of the word *health* is "uninjured, a being whole, of good omen, well, holy" (taken from the root "kailo-" according to the *American Heritage Dictionary of Indo-European Roots*). So when we look at achieving health in one dimension (for example, the physical dimension), we understand it as becoming more complete and whole in that dimension—stable and solid. We take a leap, having the courage to say, "I need to do some work on me, and I am willing to make moves to be healthier. I am ready to change."

This concrete grounding, then, gives us the opportunity to strive for that same stability and wholeness in another dimension. Though we will forever need to maintain ourselves, once we have our grounding, we continue working on our wholeness in all the other dimensions as well. Eventually—over time and with much effort—it leads us to a completeness that exudes holiness and wellness; it leads us to a place of freedom in being exactly who we are at our best. It is interesting that at its root, health is synonymous with holiness. How appropriate, then, that as we become healthier in our physical being and synchronize our physical activity with our souls, we are led to a place of greater spirituality, greater relationship with God, greater justice.

What holds you back from being healthy—whole, complete, solid, holy? What about your spirit are you afraid to look at more closely, to process more fully, to spend time contemplating, reflecting, and understanding more completely about yourself? What is it that you might be cautious to explore within these dimensions of health? We all have parts of our inner beings that we shy away from admitting and addressing—hence a sense of unhealthiness in our lives. What is it that you might be cautious to explore and why? Can you find the courage to face it? We must be OK in knowing we are not whole. We are all constantly striving for this acquisition of health (wholeness, holiness, solidity). We are constantly yearning to explode in passion.

* * *

Focusing on our physical health, gaining confidence, energy, greater fitness levels, and capability, we obtain this freedom in who we are as tangible, real beings in flesh and bone. As we become physically healthy, with confidence and pride in who we are, we have the strength and courage to face the weakness in our spiritual being. This new (or renewed) freedom then gives us the courage, power, and ability to delve into our spiritual health full-force, confident in where we come from (how far we have come), our accomplishments, and the capability to change and grow. This freedom of human being then encourages us to discover, search for, strive for, explore health and freedom in our human spirit.

Without understanding the connection between our human being and our human spirit, we cannot and will not fully grasp the magnitude of greatness that we are capable of. They are inextricably linked; finding our health and freedom in one dimension provides the support we need to explore the other. Once we find the courage to take the first step, the journey ultimately takes care of itself as we continue growing, changing, and abandoning ourselves to health in ways we likely never before imagined.

It has been my experience that the physical and spiritual dimensions of health are two of the more difficult dimensions, the two that most closely affect each other, and the two that most demand attention and taking into account the other four dimensions. The passion and freedom associated with our spiritual and physical health can completely alter how we live in the world—how we decide to spend our time, energy, and money; how we interact with other people; how we influence other people and the world at large; how we come to understand who it is that God is calling us to be and how on earth we can become that person.

* * *

In his Letter to a Young Activist, Thomas Merton said that the important question in the spiritual life is not are we happy but, rather, are we free? What does this freedom look like in our lives? What do we actually mean by freedom? Freedom achieved through health (and passion) is a place of security in who we are, where we have come from, and who we continue to become. As achieved through discovering a sound grasp on health, freedom allows us to more fully envelop ourselves in happiness, in fulfilling our dreams, and in pursuing more intentionally the persons God has made us to be. It gives us the confidence and ability to dissect the aspects of ourselves that we may not be quite content with, the pieces of our beings that we may at times be afraid, embarrassed, or scared of processing more fully.

This freedom through health makes us more powerful beings, confident in our ability to jump hurdles, climb mountains, conquer fears (literally and figuratively), and pay attention to and work on the parts of our souls that we tend to shy away from. Many of us have pieces of our spirits and souls that we are afraid to look at more closely—perhaps the fear of opening "Pandora's box" and what that will demand of us. But as we gain confidence and freedom in one part of ourselves that went from overwhelmingly scary to conquerable and manageable, we have the courage to be honest with ourselves and work on that part of our spirits, hearts, and souls that no longer seem so frightening.

* * *

Passion—both as desires/loves and as suffering—is part of this journey to freedom. If Christ's death on the cross teaches us nothing else—and I don't know how it could *not* teach us more, but if for some reason you find nothing else in the paschal mystery, I would hope you see that suffering is a part of the journey to freedom. Without Christ's death, there would be no resurrection. Without Christ's suffering, there would be no hope. Without Christ's time on the cross, we would have no salvation. Without Christ nailed to a tree, we would have no grand example of sacrifice, no understanding of the greatness of God's love for us, no true concept of who we are called to be as children of God. We would not understand the greatest of all martyrdom, and we would not see that while suffering can be redemptive, we are also mandated to work for justice on this earth so that those who inhabit our world now and in the future do not need to suffer as Christ did to obtain liberation in the future. Christ suffered and died for us so that we would have the opportunity to live lives of freedom, justice, hope, and the opportunity to fulfill our passions in service to the world.

* * *

Looking at passion in both of its definitions, we can ask ourselves, "For what am I willing to suffer?" Passion requires sacrifice and suffering while simultaneously offering us an opportunity to infuse love and joy into the world. How can we use our passion as an example to others of what it is to embrace life, strive for health, and obtain freedom? Can you—right now in this moment—imagine what it looks like to engage in your passion so intently that it leads you to that place of health (wholeness, stability, solidity, holiness) and relinquishes you into the freedom to be exactly who God calls you to be at your absolute best? Close your eyes for a few seconds and let your imagination wander. What would it look like—what would *you* look like? Who are you called to become?

EVERYBODY'S GOT A STORY

"It doesn't matter whether you…weep in darkness. It doesn't matter whether you feel loved and admired, or unloved and alone, for you are called to become a perfect creation." These are words from Edwina Gateley. In theory, I agree with her completely. Cognitively, I know that she is totally right, that whoever we are, wherever we are, however we are, we are called to become that which God had in mind when we first touched this earth (maybe even before). But try telling that to someone who is suffering, who is depressed, who feels lonely and rejected. That's when the cognitive part goes out the window, and it does very much matter whether we are weeping, whether we feel loved or unloved, and whether we feel we can continue to become.

I don't feel I can legitimately write this book and offer you my insights or reflections without sharing some of my own story and how I came to personally understand this concept of health—the journey I have walked (and continue to discover) of what it means to be in right relationship with God, myself, and others—my journey toward justice.

There was a period of about two years in my life that challenged me more than I ever imagined I could be challenged. It was a series of events that led to a seemingly permanent place of weeping, feeling unloved, and experiencing loneliness. That cognitive understanding of continuing in pursuit of my own becoming was nowhere to be seen, nowhere to be found; I was stuck in positive unhealthiness.

* * *

I had followed a job after graduate school that I thought would be perfect, that I thought would be the culmination of living my vocation. I was working for a nonprofit on the East Coast, closer to family and friends, with the chance to use lessons and skills I had learned both as a missionary and in graduate school, rooted in faith. On paper, the position could have been scripted with me in mind, and I was ecstatic. Looking back, my process of discernment was not nearly as thorough as it should have been, but I needed a job. We were in the low point of the economic crisis in the U.S., and I knew I was capable of doing well in this position. I can't say I regret my decision because I learned a lot and met some really amazing people. But if I had to go back and do it all over again, I don't know that I would do it the same way.

Have you ever been in that position? You make a decision to do something, and while you admit there were some good parts, some highlights, you also know you could probably never, ever live through the experience again, nor would you want to. And truth be told, even for all the good in it, you probably wouldn't choose it again if you had the option, knowing how difficult it was. It's a tricky balance…honoring and embracing and being grateful for the good moments in a really bad experience. I like to think those moments and those good people that came out of it was God telling me it wasn't all for naught, but at the same time, I still get somewhat angry at God when I think of how tough it was emotionally and mentally.

So I was in this job that, suffice it to say, was *not* a good situation. And in fairness, I did not handle the stress, difficulty, and toxicity of the situation well. I allowed it to seep into every other aspect of my life, letting it affect my relationships, how I spent time away from the office, my faith, my understanding of God, self, and the world. I was drinking and crying too much, exercising and sleeping too little. My prayer life was practically nonexistent. I was cutting people out of my life and was desperate for an answer about what to do to make this situation bearable or how to get out of it.

I knew within the first few weeks that it was an unhealthy situation. After months of being in this job, I received a job offer in a similar field but with less administrative responsibility, more direct service and interacting with people, and in a brand-new city where I knew no one and a state in which I had never even set foot. That opportunity for a new beginning was all I needed—I gave my two weeks' notice, packed up whatever would fit in my Honda Civic, and took off for the Lone Star State. But the damage had been done. I was beyond unhealthy and faced a long road of recuperation and recovery in pretty much every single dimension of health. I was at rock bottom, with the only saving grace being a little bit of hope for completely new and uncharted territory.

* * *

The space of absolute unhealthiness is ugly. There are different levels of unhealthiness, and I'm sure it varies from person to person. Just as being healthy will look a little different depending on your passions and heart, unhealthiness will look different depending on what triggers that downward spiral, how well you can cope, how you deal (or don't deal) with stress, how quickly you can recognize this space, and if you have the capacity, power, and opportunity to make a change.

Spiritually, it is a place of desolation. It is having no clue as to how God is present in your life, where God is acting, and how you are being guided; a lack of vision for where your life is going; and a complete absence of a sense of call and vocation, purpose, and hope. Physically, it can manifest as total apathy toward anything that might give you energy, lacking the will to care for your body through diet and/or exercise, not giving attention to what enhances your daily performance, feeling sluggish, lacking motivation to do much of anything other than sit on the couch, drown yourself in a bottle of wine, and watch the weather channel. (I wish I was exaggerating. That is how I spent more days than I care to admit.) It can be unbelievably ugly and heavy (both figuratively and literally).

Have you been there? Are you there right now? It's debilitating—a place of such depression and despair that it hurts from your head to your toes to your heart. A part of you knows that where you are is hell, but you feel completely inept to do anything about it. It's like watching a car wreck; you know it's a disaster, harmful and tragic, but you are (or feel) powerless to do anything to move in another direction. It hurts everywhere.

Do you find it a struggle to get out of bed in the morning, to exercise, to call a friend to join you for a cup of coffee? Would you rather shut yourself in your house, not deal with others, not interact with the world? Are you unmotivated to go to work, to the library, or to visit with family? Do you feel lonely, sad, like no one else in the world understands or cares? Do you feel overwhelmed and incapable of making any significant changes in your life?

I hope you have not found yourself in this place. But my guess is, more of us experience this type of unhealthiness at some point in our lives than not. And if you're there right now, in this moment, I'm sorry. I'm sorry you answered yes to the questions posed above, that you are experiencing this pain, this wretchedness, this despair that, cognitively, you wish you could respond to with urgency but that every piece of your being doesn't have the strength to even begin to confront. It is not pretty; to be quite blunt, it sucks. All I can say is that I'm sorry and I know how you feel. You are not alone.

The world can be overwhelming; life can get the best of us at times. We are human and we fail, and sometimes (as much as we want to and might even know in the back of our minds that it's there) we cannot see God's grace at work in our days. This can send us down a difficult path. It takes courage (and opportunity) to redirect ourselves, and the first step is recognizing that we are in an unhealthy situation. But that is a really big first step. So if that is where you are now, I want to encourage you in it, because you have begun the journey. You have made significant strides toward redirection, which many people are never able to do. I want to encourage you to think seriously about what your life looks like now, what you want it to look like, what God wants your life to look like, and where you might have a chance and be able to start making some changes.

* * *

For me, this unhealthiness was rooted in a job, but it infiltrated every aspect of my life: my relationships, my friendships, how I saw and experienced the world, my desire for knowledge, my motivation for anything and everything. For others, it might be rooted in an unhealthy relationship, in an experience of difficulty or depression due to a significant loss (loved one, house, job), or a situation of victimization. Any number of things can send us down a road that is unhealthy and that we allow to continue—by staying in that unhealthy relationship, by staying in that job, by not seeking some counseling or help when we know we could really use it. There is so much healing, so much health, so much freedom out there once we admit where we are and find the power within us to desire change. It may not feel like it right now, but there is a path that will take you to a place so much greater than what you can see in this moment. And this is not to say it will be easy after that first step, by any means. I don't offer this as a glimmer of hope, with rainbows and butterflies and an easy road. I offer this vision of something different, of change, of health, as someone who had to find that way. I offer it as someone who has been there and struggled.

Life will continue to bring challenges and hardship. Since this unhealthy point that I mention here, I have experienced other grave situations and difficulties. But I have faced those subsequent experiences in a much different way following that "conversion experience," if you will—my conversion into someone healthy, a conversion into someone who is proactive and continues to work on myself and not be eaten alive by the situation in which I find myself. I think about things that have happened since that time a few years ago, and I know without a doubt that had I not hit that rock bottom and found a path to health then—had I not found my freedom—it is very possible that my experiences since would have done more damage than could ever be successfully dealt with. There is hope. There is the chance to change where and how you are right now. I promise.

* * *

For me, the change started when I moved—a new city, new job, fresh start—but it was *very* gradual. As I mentioned previously, I knew but one acquaintance when I moved, a friend of a friend. We had floated in similar circles with similar people but never at the same time. Her hospitality is probably, in many cases, what saved me and brought me to a newfound state of health.

When she invited me to her Zumba class, I didn't anticipate much. I didn't anticipate finding a community of people with whom I would enjoy spending time (while doing something good for my body!); I didn't anticipate finding an outlet for my stress; I didn't anticipate finding a form of exercise that would allow me to lose significant weight; I didn't anticipate finding a subsequent love and passion for dance; I didn't anticipate finding a new career; I didn't anticipate finding my way back to relationships that had once been so life-giving and would become so again; I didn't anticipate finding a new piece of my heart, soul, and identity that would lead to a complete life overhaul. I found all of the above, and then some.

I started going to my friend's Zumba class a few times a week. She had such a passion and love for the music and movement—it really was contagious and infectious. She loved to dance, and I started tagging along when she invited me out socially as well. After a while, I started going out dancing on my own as well, and then decided to take a salsa class to actually learn the steps. I began to structure my days around the Zumba program and salsa. (I was still new to the city, so I didn't have much else going on.) Zumba fitness didn't even feel like exercise—it just felt like I was hanging out with friends and truly losing myself for an hour at a time in a totally new and exciting adventure of music and dance and sweat and laughter. (If you've never taken a Zumba class, they are often ripe with laughter. Pretty much everyone, including the instructor, feels like a fool at some point as you move your feet, arms, and hips in sometimes crazy flailing motions.) Her constant invitation (and encouragement) allowed me to discover this new hobby—which rather quickly turned into a passion.

* * *

After taking classes for a number of months, having successfully lost more than twenty pounds by practicing Zumba fitness alone, and at my friend's encouragement, I decided to get certified as an instructor. Let's be clear: I had no intention of teaching—zero, zilch, none whatsoever. I was in a job that, while I didn't 100 percent love it, I was comfortable. Zumba fitness was just something I had come to love to do, and quite honestly, my number-one reason for getting certified was that I thought it would make a phenomenal ice breaker. Have you ever played the game "two truths and a lie" when you're with a new group of people? I have played this game often in different groups, and I thought for sure I'd be able to use "certified Zumba instructor" as one of my two truths that would stump people. God really does work in mysterious ways.

After finding out I was certified, my salsa teacher, who had become a friend and owned a Latin-dance studio, asked me if I would be interested in teaching just one class a week, just for fun. I ended up saying yes, for no other reason than I thought, *I don't really have any reason not to…it's not like I'm doing anything else.* So I started teaching one class a week. One class a week turned into two, and two turned into three. Before I knew it, I was one of the main Zumba instructors at this Latin-dance studio. I was going out dancing socially, and the salsa "regulars" at the club knew exactly which song to grab me for. I was amazed. People who didn't even necessarily know my name knew how to challenge me and push me outside of my comfort zone on the dance floor. One gentleman I used to dance with frequently when I first started going out (a retired salsa instructor), who didn't know my name, said to me one night during a much faster salsa than I was used to, "Stop being afraid. Let yourself go, give in to the music, and be pushed outside of your comfort zone. You can't always stick with what you know." He was talking to me about my life at large just as much as he was talking about my dancing. It was in such moments that I knew God had me here for a reason and that the Holy Spirit was at work.

Have you experienced that—someone you barely know, an acquaintance, or classmate says something so clearly on target you feel as though he or she is looking directly into your soul and touching the absolute depths of your heart? Those are the moments when we have to know something—someone—greater is out there. They are moments of grace; in my opinion, those are the moments when God is so very clearly using someone in our lives to tell us something. Dare we not pay attention?

* * *

Things were good, and I was hooked on this focus on my physical health. However, I had stopped seeing significant physical changes through Zumba class, so I decided to participate in some boot-camp classes a few mornings a week. There I found yet another amazing community of people who served as incredible accountability partners. We worked out together multiple early mornings a week, and if I missed a class, I got a text message or post asking why I wasn't there. I grew to really appreciate these people, who became more of a support and challenge system than I ever imagined I would find in a new city, much less through doing pushups and planks and salamanders (which, for the record, are the bane of my existence—least favorite exercise ever).

As I continued in these forms of exercise, I became more and more aware of my body and what I was and didn't want to be putting into it. I chose foods that were better for me, I drank a lot less, I got more sleep, and in general just cared more for myself. I drank more water, ate more fruit, went for a run on the days I didn't have a Zumba class or boot camp. I was becoming stronger, more confident, more grounded, happier. I lost weight, gained confidence, read more books, and the people with whom I worked and interacted started to see me as an example. At work, I was known as the health nut (if only they had seen me just months before). At boot camp, I was known as the Zumba instructor. At Zumba class, I was known as the instructor with a success story that others hoped would become their own. Before I knew it, physically, I was *healthy*.

* * *

For everything I had gained in my physical health, I hadn't gained anything spiritually speaking. I was still in my job, and after a year I was pushed into yet another administrative position, which brought with it new insights to the inner workings of this nonprofit. (Yes, another nonprofit position. You'd think I would have learned a lesson, but sometimes we don't clue in quickly enough.) This new role was accompanied by an inner circle of injustice, both in how I witnessed others being treated and in how I was being treated. It wasn't nearly as bad as the position I had previously held, but I wouldn't say it was good either. I didn't know what to do. I wasn't willing to uproot my life again. I loved its other aspects: Zumba classes, salsa, the friends I had made, the newfound love for fitness, health, and wellness. I didn't want to give up any of that, but I also didn't want to stay somewhere that had the potential of drawing me back into a dark space of desolation and unhealthiness. I was wary of anything that would cause me to regress, and I must admit that as such, I had a bit of my guard up.

I continued doing what I was doing and tried to do it well. I was also putting feelers out there for what my life could look like if it was time for a change. Obviously, administrative roles in international nonprofits are not my forte. (Either that or I just had really poor luck with the organizations I had chosen to work for. In all honesty, I think it was a little bit of both.) I had continued in good relationship with my friend and boss, the owner of the Latin-dance studio, and she had shared with me her dreams of expanding the studio and eventually branching out into a community nonprofit that would focus on offering healthy opportunities for exercise and dance to single moms who struggled financially and physically. This sounded amazing to me, and I spent time thinking about what I would need to do to be of use in such a situation.

I honestly don't know when or how I decided to pursue certification as a personal trainer, but that's where I found myself. By day I was directing a faith-based nonprofit—quite a farce when I stop to think about it: I was still in this place of spiritual desolation. I had worked hard toward and achieved a solid place of health physically. But spiritually, I was unfulfilled, uncertain, lacking purpose, lacking the assuredness of God's presence in my life. I hadn't yet made it out of the space of desolation into which

I had plunged during my prior position. And yet here I was, talking about faith on a daily basis, accompanying others spiritually, offering spiritual guidance, challenging others to go deeper into their understanding of God, liberation theology, Christ among those who live in material poverty, Christ among themselves, and so forth. I was inauthentic, spiritually speaking, and I knew that was not a good place for me or for those with whom I was working. So I threw myself into my "night job"—choreographing Zumba songs, paying attention to the trainers I worked with, studying anatomy, nutrition, joint movements, anaerobic and aerobic energy systems, interval training and goal-specific training techniques. I took the exam and became a certified personal trainer through the Aerobics and Fitness Association of America.

* * *

This "success," for lack of a better term, in the physical-health realm was empowering. I felt strong, capable, and confident. I had come such a long way on this journey to physical health and had come to recognize the importance of fitness, diet, nutrition, and exercise. It had been a transformative experience, and while I was at this crossroads in my professional life, I knew I wanted to share this journey with others and walk with people on their own journey to health and wellness. The desires of my heart that I had longed for in my nonprofit jobs—to help others, to walk with others, to accompany others on a transformative journey—were still imprinted deeply on my heart. That piece of my passion hadn't changed. Instead of walking with others on a spiritual journey as I had always thought I was called to do, maybe I was really called to walk with them on the physical journey toward health. Maybe I was being called to use my own experience, my struggle with weight loss and body image and strength and conditioning to guide others along a similar path. I had a passion for exercise, for learning more about how the body works and how we can better care for ourselves. The girl who had barely scraped by in tenth-grade biology was now finding a true desire to walk with and guide others in their understanding of how exercise affects our bodies and benefits our physical being. Particularly living in a city that was the second most obese in the United States at the time, where diabetes was/is at an all-time high, and many people suffer from major health problems due to poor eating habits and a sedentary lifestyle, I was seeing this opportunity as an immense gift to address needs in the world around me. I was healthy, I was free, and it was leading me to a vocation.

* * *

In a course of events that can only be described as divine intervention, connections and networking led me to discover a temporary part-time position in ministry at a local Catholic university focused on social justice (one of my areas of interest and expertise, given my experiences as a missionary and my studies in graduate school). There was no coincidence here—God was clearly at work, which I could see even in my then-current space of spiritual desolation. (Looking back, recognizing God's presence in it all at the time was probably the beginning of my spiritual turning point.) I thought, *Well, Clare, here's your chance. Do both. Follow this passion for health, fitness, and the physically transformative journey of others, and spend some time this next year ministering in the spiritual-health realm as well. Take this year as a year of discernment—where are you being called? What are you being called to become? It's going to be difficult—juggling multiple part-time jobs in two different areas of ministry and accompaniment and expertise and not being in any salaried positions. But if you don't do it now, you'll never know.* I'd much rather regret something I've done than something I didn't do. I gave my two weeks' notice at the nonprofit.

* * *

I found myself teaching nine Zumba classes a week, recruiting and training clients one on one, and spending twenty hours a week in social-justice ministry at the university. But I was still nervous it wouldn't be enough; nonprofit jobs don't pay extraordinarily well, but I had always managed to cover my bases. With these part-time jobs, I was worried that I'd be cutting it far too close for comfort (or, better said, too close to not making my student-loan payments). As God would have it (some might say luck, but I know better), a position fell into my lap to teach at the same university at which I was ministering. I took on a position as adjunct faculty in the Exercise and Sports Science department, teaching a core, basic class: the bare bones of anatomy (no pun intended!), kinesiology, the basics of movement, and how our students are and will be so unique in their vocations because of their Catholic education. Their skill set and intellectual knowledge may well be quite similar to those of their future colleagues coming from a wide variety of educational institutions. But our students are different because of the unique education they receive in Catholic tradition and our specific charism.

I also found myself able to take this leap of faith because, at the same time that I was transitioning into these new positions, I moved into an intentional community. Sharing life, space, and finances with another person (and later, as we would add a third to our group, another two people), gave me the confidence to take this chance on something I had no idea how it would turn out. My community provided a safe space to make this jump, knowing that I had a safety net that would cradle me if I was in over my head. Our community came into existence through a number of other grace-filled moments and Spirit-driven circumstances, but that's another story for another day. The backing of my community to take this chance was like the last piece to the puzzle that ended up reading: Go. Do it. Make the leap. Take a chance on faith. Believe.

* * *

The year of discernment, part-time work, juggling the balance between ministering to students spiritually, training clients, teaching Zumba fitness (ministering to people in their physical journey), and living in community was one of the hardest—and most rewarding—years. It was exhausting, unquestionably, to juggle so many jobs, to have so much of my necessary income dependent on my own physical health, and to be constantly in positions of ministry that required me to be "on my game," so to speak (energetic in Zumba class, challenging in the classroom, empathetic in ministry, encouraging yet demanding with my training clients).Through it, I found God so incredibly present in how it all fell into place and how I found the stamina to persist. I could never in my wildest dreams have imagined that I would have any of these jobs (vocations), and here I was doing not one thing that fit me but four! For the first time in many years, I was happy in the work I was doing; I could see my purpose as it fit into the picture of the kingdom God calls us to work for here on earth, and I was confident in my calling. It was completely, unquestionably providential, and I was constantly being affirmed that this was exactly where God was calling me. I was helping others, I was walking with others physically and spiritually. I was being continuously formed and challenged and affirmed in my own health—in both dimensions—and continuing to grow into the person I am called to become.

* * *

I never would have been able to land these jobs if not for finding a passion in fitness and exercise that led me to a place of concrete physical health. And I never would have taken such a large leap of faith—to quit a stable job to try my hand at brand-new adventures that were completely outside of my previous experience and expertise—if not for the confidence in who God created me to be that came with the freedom of having become physically healthy. The physical journey I experienced led me to a place of being able to believe that God has a greater plan for me, and I but need the strength to follow it, even if it seems the most unlikely, uncommon, or unconventional of choices. Achieving a solid state of health through Zumba fitness, exercise, and training made me open to the possibilities that awaited me spiritually. That leap of faith was pivotal in my journey of wellness—that is, being healthy *and* happy.

That year of multiple jobs and discernment led me to where I am now. I still do all four of those things (I just do less of some and more of others now). I know God calls me to spiritual ministry, rooted in social justice and Catholic social teaching. Teaching in the Exercise and Sports Science department gives me the opportunity to talk about and engage with others in this idea of health in multiple dimensions and how interconnected they are. No one dimension can be lived in isolation, but often we do need to focus on one first so as to find ourselves in the others. I continue to train clients (fewer of them now), and I love the one-on-one relationships that I have the gift of building with those with whom I work. I teach a few Zumba classes a week. I honestly cannot imagine my life without this program. Not only is it so much a part of my own personality and identity now, but I often still need it, to lose myself in the music and the sweat and at times escape a heavy day. I am not perfect, and my own journey of fitness, health, and wellness continues.

I am not completely healthy all the time. I exercise regularly, I thank God daily, and I try to get enough sleep (some days are better than others). I procrastinate and will often choose to choreograph a new song when I should be grading quizzes. I spend time with others but could probably work a little less and socialize a little more. I pray regularly but often don't have enough patience for God's timing. I struggle at times to find balance in relationships—having recently gotten married, being involved in various communities, and maintaining friendships from other times and places in my life. I am not nearly slow enough to anger or rich enough in kindness. I definitely don't read as many books as I would like or know enough about current global events. I eat ice cream and I drink wine (in moderation, but probably more than I should on both accounts). I am faced with challenges and sometimes unwelcome experiences, but I have learned ways to cope, deal with stress, and ask for help.

I am healthy and happy—I am well, but it is a never-ending journey, and there will never be a day where that is not a conscious choice I have to make. I must continue to choose, every day, to see grace and to seize the opportunity for growth. There will never be a day where I will not have to make a commitment, every morning, to becoming who I am called to be and to being well.

CAREFUL...YOU MIGHT CATCH IT

The choice to be healthy leads to freedom, but what does this "freedom" mean? What does it mean to live free? In some ways, we can look at freedom through the lens of what it's not: Freedom is not being confined to one specific thing. Freedom is not being limited in our choices and opportunities. Freedom is not being told exactly what to do and having to follow it for fear of punishment. Freedom is not experiencing the constraints of a specific way, a particular manner, of walking down a mandated path. Freedom is openness. Freedom is having the ability to choose—what we do, how we react, where we thrive. Freedom is health, freedom is happiness, freedom is being well and sharing our wellness with others.

I spent a summer in Cameroon, a small country in West Africa, working on my thesis and experiencing new ways of living, learning, and being. It was a wonderful experience, different from what I expected it to be and full of both challenge and joy. One phrase I heard often in southern Cameroon is, "You are free." The phrase is used in a myriad of contexts, from asking permission to do something to being dismissed from the dinner table to a response to liking something and its being offered to you. I lived with a large, beautiful, wonderful family during my time there, and my host sister used this phrase often, but it never seemed to lose its impact on me.

What powerful words—"You are free." Indeed, I am free. I have journeyed to discover my passions. I continue to find new aspects of health and wellness that enhance my overall being. I have wonderful friends and loved ones who encourage me to be in my own skin, to be who I am (even if that person is oftentimes not what society would deem as a "normal" young adult taking the prescribed path), and to grow and love openly and unabashedly. I am fortunate to have been born into a situation where I have had access to a good education and a wealth of opportunity. I have had the chance to try new things and find out what I don't enjoy just as much as what I do enjoy. I have had the liberty to follow my passions and discover my vocation.

I have worked on and continue to make efforts to maintain my physical health through activities that brighten my days, make me smile, invite me to sweat (a lot!), allow me to be in community with others who care about engaging in a proactive approach to good health. Through that, I have had the freedom to discover how other aspects of health are manifested in my life; I have been free to be part of an intentional community, to talk about faith over dinner, to pray openly for those I know and those I don't know, to share my spiritual journey and continue to be pushed to know God more. I have had the freedom to love others, even those who consider themselves unlovable. I've had the opportunity on multiple occasions to learn to love in a new language, in a new culture, in foreign lands, and to let that love transform me. I have been gifted with the ability to dedicate my life to living my faith through efforts for justice and equality. I can be exactly who I am—the good, the bad, and the aspects that can constantly be challenged to change—and do so without fear of rejection, abandonment, or too much distress. I am indeed free, and I continue to grow into my freedom.

Are you free? Do you do what you love and do it well? Are you able to live your passions in a way that brings you into greater, deeper relationship with God and others? Do you feel confident in how you spend your days, in your ability to make a decision, in how you choose to spend your time, money, and energy? Do you make good, conscious decisions that lead you to a place of better health and wholeness, that give you further insight into the stirrings of your heart and soul, your joys and sources of light and life in your days? Are you yourself, the you God created you to be, with all your strengths and weaknesses, flaws and faults, the gifts you bring into the world that are unique and specific? Are you honest with yourself and your loved ones, letting your true colors shine, letting your naked face be seen, letting others into your heart and entering into the hearts of others? Do you trust the movement of the Spirit? Do you believe in God's grace? Do you work for the presence of justice in your life? Are you free?

* * *

My college roommate had a quote she loved to return to often and challenged me to constantly think about: "Life is change, growth is optional. Choose wisely." Sometimes things in life happen that we don't have much control over. But we always have the opportunity to choose growth; regardless whether things that happen are good or bad, how we react is within our control. We can choose to get through things or grow through things; we can choose to focus on the bad and the difficult in life or choose to look for God's grace and focus on positivity. We can shy away from challenge or accept and embrace it; we can choose not to believe or to trust and believe in that which we have not seen. We can hate or we can love; we can choose isolation or justice; we can choose discord or peace and harmony. We can doubt or choose to live in hope; we can stay still or we can choose to make moves. The latter of all of these situations requires us to make conscious decisions, real choices, and intentional selections day in and day out.

This journey toward wellness requires day after day, moment after moment, that we choose growth. This choice of growth leads to a more profound space and place—where our freedom is overwhelming and our passions are contagious.

* * *

Contagious passion. What does this mean exactly? It's not forcing others into passion, growth, health, freedom. It's an invitation—but an invitation that others simply cannot find it within themselves to decline as they *choose* to join you on the journey. When we see someone happy, joyful, fulfilled, and passionate, we want the same; we want it for ourselves, and we want to share it with others. But we can't do the exact same thing another did; we can't find our passion necessarily in the same place or in the same amount of time or in the same manner another did. We are each unique and special, and God works in our lives in different ways that respond to the truth of each of our hearts.

This contagious passion, the spreading of health and happiness, can't come from jealousy or competition. We can't invite others onto the path because we want people to boost our ego or tell us we're great, and likewise we can't join another on the journey because we want to be like them or want to be better than they are.

I love being a Zumba instructor. I don't just love it because I get to lose myself in the music, get a good workout, move my body in different and fun patterns to amazing rhythms, enjoy sweating, or can challenge my body to perform at the next level. I don't just love teaching because I get to see community grow, watch a large group of people move together without even realizing what a beautiful reality they create, because people have fun and look forward to spending an hour together moving to music they might not otherwise have ever heard before.

Indeed, these aforementioned aspects are part of why I love my role as a Zumba instructor, but I love it too because it gives me the gift of watching and walking with others as they discover a passion and set out on their own journey toward freedom. I have watched some students lose fifty pounds, finding new confidence and levels of self-esteem they never imagined they would possess. I have watched people who have never danced a single step discover a love for movement and music. I have watched a young woman who had never taken a Zumba class before fall so in love with it that she went on to become an instructor. I have watched the smiles and the laughter that have come with people being in class and losing all inhibitions and embracing attempts at steps they have never seen. I have witnessed people conquer and more than prove wrong society's opinion that they are "too old for this." I have seen people make new friends. I have seen people for whom, through Zumba class, new parts of their hearts have come alive—they interact with their families differently, they find joy in new activities, they live more fully, breathe more deeply, and smile more genuinely. They find happiness in smaller things—and I don't just mean their pants fitting more loosely (though that happens all too often). Being a Zumba instructor is a huge gift that I cannot imagine not embracing.

Zumba fitness, however, is not for everyone, and that's OK. Some people love lifting weights, some love cycling, others love yoga. My goal is not to convert everyone I meet into a Zumba lover. Although I appreciate yoga—I go to a yoga class maybe fifteen to twenty times a year to try to regain some balance and give my body a rest from jumping and dancing and confuse my muscles once in a while—I know that I could not get my daily exercise fix from something so…well, quiet. It's just not me. Likewise, I fully understand that not everyone likes to exercise to blaring music, bright colors, fast movement, and Latin rhythms. My goal is to encourage others to find their passions, live them into health, and let that health carry them into freedom.

Once that freedom starts to grow in your heart, it is invasive and pervasive, intoxicating and addicting, and you want to feel that freedom in all you are and in all you do—you want that freedom in your physical existence as much as in your spiritual. It's wonderful, and the great news is—unlike other things that can be addicting and intoxicating—it's so incredibly good for you and good for our world. I have a number of friends who find this freedom, this elation, in running. They often describe it as a "runner's high," and once you have experienced that high, you take to the trails or road time and time again; you cannot imagine not getting that high. Your endorphins are peaking and you are literally taken to another world.

Have you ever felt this way during exercise? It can happen in an instant—a switch is thrown, and suddenly you go from wanting to wipe your sweat away and sit down to a remarkable new place where you cannot express your joy. You can't smile enough, you can't run fast enough, you can't put any more effort into your move because you are literally giving it everything you've got and you are loving every millisecond of it. Your heart wants to burst—not from your rapid heart rate, but from joy and bliss. You're hooked. And it's this feeling of indescribable happiness that will keep you coming back. Because ultimately, it's just too good to go without for very long. It is passion in its purest, most unadulterated, most intensely wonderful form; it's tangible, so real, so joyful, so sweaty that you can taste it. Do you know what I'm talking about? If you do, then you know that few words are capable of really describing the emotion of that moment. If not, what is keeping you from finding your passion? What is keeping you from being free?

* * *

This passion is so real and so viral, you can catch it from another. It's about doing what you love and inviting others into the joy. It's about making this passion contagious and showing outwardly what an amazing experience is happening inwardly. It's about moving—some of the most basic and fundamental activities and actions of the human body—and moving in a way that is not only beautiful and natural but that expresses the truth in your heart. Professional (ballet) dancer and author Mary Ellen Hunt said, "Remember that dance has a dimension beyond the physical. The body—as imperfect as it always is—is only part of the picture. Your energy, the quality of your movement, your feeling about the world, your dance spirit—that is what we see under the lights."

To fully grasp what is at the heart of a true Zumba instructor, I would couple Mary Ellen's words with those of Rodney Yee, advanced yoga instructor, yoga studio owner, and author. (For more information, visit yeeyoga.com.) Yee says, "I can inspire you, but you have to sweat your own prayer." Exploring the dimensions of being—including but not limited to the physical—and inspiring others to sweat their own prayer is what Zumba fitness, at its best, is about. The movement, the physical exertion, the sweat, is just the beginning of this freedom. Your physical actions lead to the unleashing of this spirit, of this passion—they lead to a space of freedom to not speak but rather to move, bend, sweat, run, jump, dance, and let your action be your prayer. Let your body communicate the joy of your heart.

* * *

One of the key phrases you will hear/see from the Zumba crew is "Love to Live. Live to Party!" It may sound cheesy to some, but it's true. Think about it: love to live. Life is meant to be lived, lived well, and lived rooted in love. This love comes from those right relationships—with God, self, and others—truly living our days to their fullest, in as genuine and beautiful a way as possible, trying to do good and spread joy to all with whom we come in contact. Now, living to party—or perhaps better said, seeing life as a party—can have a deeper meaning than we might originally think.

Henri Nouwen, who in my opinion is one of the greatest spiritual writers of all time, spent a good deal of time with those who are poor. At times, he accompanied those who were materially poor (like the time he spent in Bolivia and Peru); at times, he accompanied those who were physically poor (the years he spent committed to the L'Arche community). And throughout these experiences he wrote about what he learned, experienced, reflected on, and how it all influenced his own prayer and spirituality. In his *¡Gracias! A Latin American Journal,* Nouwen says, "Gratitude is one of the most visible characteristics of the poor I have come to know. This all-pervading gratitude is the basis for celebration. Not only are the poor grateful for life, but they also *celebrate life constantly*....All of life is a gift, a gift to be celebrated, a gift to be shared. Thus the poor are Eucharistic people, people who know to say thanks be to God, to life, to each other...for them, *all of life is a long fiesta with God.*"

Now, I recognize that for some, this might be a stretch. My paralleling Henri Nouwen's reflection on his experience with those who are materially poor in Latin America and Zumba fitness's motto of "Live to Party!" might seem practically sacrilegious to some. But I think there's something deeper here. In both cases, we are talking about a more profound experience of celebrating life. We are talking about experiencing a not-only-human dynamic but a spark of the divine in both cases. We are talking about celebrating in community, loving life in the presence of others, refocusing on the simple basics of goodness in our world...whether that means sitting on a stoop and breathing in the dust of the roads and the air of the Third World or letting your body feel free to move as the music calls it and the sweat runs down your brow. It's about searching for optimal health, following your passion, and experiencing freedom; we are talking about recognizing, embracing, and appreciating the simple gift that is being on this earth, that is being alive, and—God willing—being well.

* * *

Stripping ourselves of the chaos, materialism, technology, societal pressures, expectations expressed by media, and the "shoulds" that exist all around us—stepping back from the demands of the external world—allows us an opportunity to spend time on what really matters. Maybe we step away from all of this in quiet prayer or maybe by praying with a community or maybe by volunteering regularly at a local nonprofit. These are ways to refocus our spiritual beings. Physically, perhaps we step away from the pressures and demands all around us by going for a run, attending Zumba class regularly, spending the first hour of every weekday committed to our yoga practice. These are all ways of removing ourselves from the world to refocus, to listen to God's whispers in our hearts, to indeed center ourselves on the vital parts of our lives that require our attention most. And what are these parts, what really matters? Well, health, certainly, as we first defined it—being in right relationship with God, self, and others. I would also offer that these relationships allow us to get to the heart of our existence—thanking God, living in, appreciating, and embracing the moment in which we can hold in our hands, hearts, minds, and souls the beauty of this blessed world and our place in it.

How do you celebrate life? Where do you find yourself being able to step back from being of the world and focusing instead on your presence in the world and the goodness you have to offer—rooted in a spirituality and strength that counterculturally challenges the status quo? What makes you love to live? For what do you thank God, and how do you express your gratitude? What prayer do you sweat?

* * *

It is through these opportunities to celebrate and give thanks—both in prayer and action—that we build community. Community—an unbelievably powerful group of people rooted in faith, rooted in Christian love, that strives to mirror Jesus' presence on earth. Christ inspired others to be the best version of themselves that they could possibly be. He wanted them to recognize the person that God created in God's own image and likeness and to constantly strive to be that person—ever growing, ever adapting, ever challenging, ever more humble, ever more powerful. The power of community comes not from one specific person or source; rather, as we influence one another, as we grow and change and learn and love, we become, collectively, a more clear reflection of the body of Christ, encouraging one another along the way.

In his First Letter to the Corinthians, Saint Paul says, "As a body is one though it has many parts, and all the parts of the body, though many, are one body, so also Christ. For in one Spirit we were all baptized into one body, whether Jews or Greeks, slaves or free persons, and we were all given to drink of one Spirit. Now the body is not a single part, but many. If a foot should say, 'Because I am not a hand I do not belong to the body,' it does not for this reason belong any less to the body. Or if an ear should say, 'Because I am not an eye I do not belong to the body,' it does not for this reason belong any less to the body. If the whole body were an eye, where would the hearing be? If the whole body were hearing, where would the sense of smell be? But as it is, God placed the parts, each one of them, in the body as he intended. If they were all one part, where would the body be? But as it is, there are many parts, yet one body. The eye cannot say to the hand, 'I do not need you,' nor again the head to the feet, 'I do not need you.' Indeed, the parts of the body that seem to be weaker are all the more necessary, and those parts of the body that we consider less honorable we surround with greater honor, and our less presentable parts are treated with greater propriety, whereas our more presentable parts do not need this. But God has so constructed the body as to give greater honor to a part that is without it, so that there may be no division in the body, but that the parts may have the same concern for one another. If [one] part suffers, all the parts suffer with it; if one part is honored, all the parts share its joy. Now you are Christ's body, and individually parts of it" (12:12–27).

We need one another to make this world even close to what it can be, to come close to God's vision for the world. Each person has a unique set of talents, skills, joy, passion, likes, energy—and without all of those coming together in efforts to bring to fruition the making real of a shared vision, we would be nowhere. We would be living an isolated existence, operating out of a complete silo. There is a major difference between existing and living. One can exist simply by a physical presence on this earth. That presence might be unhealthy, it might be harmful to others, it might be hindered by the society in which one lives, it might be full of difficulty, of injustice—hunger, malnutrition, illness, material poverty, emotional poverty, spiritual poverty. It might be a presence that brings no sense of joy or purpose. There is no focus on why we are here, how we can grow and challenge or positively impact the space and place in which we live. It is not a call to more fully grasp one's personhood; there is no focus on the development of the soul. It is purely and only existing, having a body that has weight and occupies a small piece of the atmosphere and takes in oxygen—nothing more.

Now, living—that's a whole nother story. Living is what we refer to when we are talking about health. When we talk about relationship and freedom and passion, when we talk about hope and challenge and joy and sorrow, when we speak of growth and faith and wholeness and community, when we focus on ways to improve ourselves and the world around us, discovery and vocation and questioning the ways of the world and our own roles in the world—that is when we are talking about *living*.

Take a moment to think about these distinctions. Are you

existing, or are you living? Do you encourage others to live, and live well? Without the presence of one another, of community, we would never know to what extent we can make Christ's presence visible in this world. Without encouraging one another in the discovery of passion and the living into freedom of our own gifts, health, and relationships, we would not make tangible the goodness that comes from our being. We need one another to be whole, to be well. We need a friend to invite us into the discovery of something new and beautiful. Yee's students need him to lead them into their yoga practice, to sweat their prayer. My Zumba students need me to be smiling and loving what I do when we are forty minutes into the class and their hearts are pounding from the cardiovascular rigor they are enduring. We need others to help us find health, our passions, and freedom. And then, in a very basic "pay it forward" method, we need to help those we encounter do the same. Just as my host sister often reminded me in Cameroon, we need to constantly remind and encourage one another: "You are free."

* * *

In this encouraging of one another into freedom, we simultaneously invite those with whom we interact to let their own beauty, freedom, and living presence be a remarkable gift to this world. By embracing and engaging our own freedom and truth in our daily tasks, conversations, and activities, we give the example to others to do the same, and serve as examples for the multitude of ways in which we bring love and light to the world. As we grow into our own gifts and the talents and characteristics that we uniquely offer the world, we take that light within us, shine it brightly, and make space for those around us to do likewise, to join us in being a brighter, stronger, more powerful light for the world.

How do you shine? How do you live your freedom so well that

you manifest the glory of God within you and subsequently encourage others to do the same? How do you join with others on this journey to being a collective body of Christ, to living in freedom, to growth and love and gratitude and celebration? How do others encourage you to shine, and how do you pay that forward?

Freedom, for all that it is, certainly is not free—meaning, we don't just "get it." We work for it; we go through long journeys of health and suffering and passion and hard work to get to our freedom. And that's just in one dimension of health: we finally achieve our freedom in our physical health, where we live our passions and love to focus on exercise, nutrition, and energy levels, just to turn around and start the journey from scratch in our spiritual-health dimension, now combined with maintenance and working at balance. Not only does the journey become more intricate for us in our own right, but once we're there, we also have the responsibility of inviting others to freedom. But that's the easy part, inviting others in, because the domino effect can be pretty amazing—this freedom, just as passion, is contagious. Think back to how we described this experience of freedom within the context of health: being in a remarkable place where you cannot sufficiently express your joy. You can't smile enough, you are literally giving everything you've got, and you are loving every millisecond of it. Your heart wants to burst from joy and bliss. It's the feeling of indescribable happiness; it is passion in its purest, most unadulterated, most intensely wonderful form. How could people not want in when they see these manifestations in another?

It is a responsibility that is both a gift and a necessary task—it is part of the package. And just as we don't easily acquire this freedom that comes through health, neither will those with whom we walk the journey. But our example, our joy, and our love for God, self, and the world (I bet!) will be so enticing that others can't help but want to find their freedom too.

LET'S EXAMINE (AND EXAMEN)

I t's often very easy, upon seeing something beautiful and tempting (that is, the joy associated with health and freedom), to say, "I want that. There is where I want to be." Getting there—that's an entirely different story. Recognizing your own need and desire for greater health and balance, thinking about the joy that comes with engaging in your passions and finding subsequent freedom, you may now find yourself wondering, "Where do I begin?" We have to know that the journey will take time, and we must be patient; we will experience successes and failures, and it will not all be a smooth ride. But we've all got to start somewhere, and asking ourselves "Where?" is the first step.

I believe Ignatian spirituality offers us an array of useful tools for our faith development, discernment, and spiritual growth. Saint Ignatius of Loyola and the Jesuits (the Society of Jesus) have contributed in great magnitude to the basis of Catholic thought and reflection, offering opportunities for both religious and laypeople to focus more significantly on the calling to be "contemplatives in action" and find avenues to live our faith through justice more concretely in the modern world. Let's first begin with a little bit of background to the process in which I will invite you to try to find your first step.

* * *

Saint Ignatius developed what are known as the Spiritual Exercises. The Spiritual Exercises combine a mixture of prayers, points of meditation, and various contemplative practices that invite us into the deepening of our relationship with God. Many vowed Jesuits (as well as other religious, and on rare occasion, laypeople who can get the time off) will embark on a thirty-day silent retreat to engage in the Exercises. Recently, in an effort to make the Spiritual Exercises more accessible to laypeople, they have been modified so as to allow people to move through them via a month-long program of daily prayer and meeting with a spiritual director.

When I was a senior in college, I went on a five-day silent retreat built upon the Spiritual Exercises. It was a challenge for me—first, the challenge of being silent for such a perceived long period of time; and second, it was a challenge to truly make myself vulnerable to this practice of prayer and be willing to enter fully into the reflections and discernment that came from this experience. At the time, I was discerning the call to post-graduate service in Latin America, and looking back, it was one of the best possible ways I could have engaged in so as to truly hear where God was calling me.

It was scary at moments to tune in to the stirrings of my heart and be open to God's presence in my life, but through prayer and the assistance of my spiritual director while on retreat, I found the faith and courage to embrace this countercultural choice upon my graduation from college. In a society where we are constantly bombarded with the importance of an education purely to obtain a job and make a lot of money, it goes against the grain to choose not to immediately get a job and make money but to move to another country, receive no compensation for work, and live in a Christ-centered community with other young adults spending time daily in prayer and shared meals. At the time, only about 1 percent of my graduating class from college (a Jesuit university) went on to spend time in long-term service. We were choosing an unlikely path, much to the chagrin of those who thought we would be "wasting our time" or putting our chances of getting a good job in jeopardy. But part of truly engaging in the Spiritual

Exercises, in my experience, was the empowerment to give myself completely over to the will of God.

* * *

In my opinion, one of the most beautiful prayers of all time is Saint Ignatius's *Suscipe*:

> Take, Lord, and receive all my liberty,
> my memory, my understanding,
> and my entire will,
> all I have and call my own.
>
> You have given all to me.
> To you, Lord, I return it.
>
> Everything is yours; do with it what you will.
> Give me only your love and your grace, that is enough for me.

This prayer, the *Suscipe* (which is the Latin word for "receive"), sketches out for us the ultimate purpose of life—to surrender to God's will, to rely solely on God's love and grace, to source our lives from the knowledge and understanding that all we have—our one and only life—is a gift we receive from God. The Spiritual Exercises give us an opportunity to more fully comprehend this fact and to contemplate and reflect on how we live our days as manifestations of God's love and grace.

Here is where we can begin to take the first step, begin to figure out where we are and where we need/want to be. One of the gems that have come from the Jesuits and their devotion to the teachings of Saint Ignatius of Loyola has been that of the daily examen of conscience. Thinking about ways in which we can continuously reflect on our ability to live in a place of spiritual health and wellness, the daily examen of conscience can be a wonderful tool.

Particularly for those of us who might not be sure exactly "where we are spiritually" or how to begin to look for areas of growth in our own spiritual health, the daily examen can give us a valuable framework to engage with in reflection.

For Ignatius, praying the examen twice daily was one of his few rules of prayer. There are a number of adaptations of the examen, different methods that can be employed, all with the purpose of reflecting on the day to detect God's presence and discern God's will for us. Ignatius considered the examen to be a direct gift from God, which could not be absent in one's daily spiritual life.

The most common form of praying with the examen of conscience involves spending time in quiet (for most laypeople, usually done at night, before bed) and reflecting on five different points:

- Become aware of God's presence.
- Review the day with gratitude.
- Pay attention to your emotions.
- Choose one feature of the day and pray from it.
- Look toward tomorrow.

Through this examen of conscience, we are invited to reflect on the various aspects of our day: recognizing the greater Being at work in our world; being attentive to the sources of joy and the sources of sorrow in our days; the ways in which we succeeded to live God's will for us, served God, and the ways in which we failed God; giving thanks for moments of grace and the ability to recognize God's presence in our days; reflecting on the ways in which we can do better tomorrow. All prayerful reflection comes from a place of gratitude, being thankful for the moments (of both joy and struggle) that God places in our lives.

* * *

One critical aspect of this practice is being open and vulnerable to our failings. Failing is not a bad thing; failing gives us the chance to recognize not necessarily what our weaknesses are but, rather, what areas invite us into growth. During my second year as a volunteer in Ecuador, I was part of a wonderful community. (Note: wonderful doesn't mean happy or easy; wonderful means we came together to witness Christ's presence in our world and challenged one another—challenge rooted in deep and profound Christian love—to become more whole, faith-filled beings and agents of change in our world.) Every night at 6:30 PM, our community sat down to dinner together, and every night at 6:30 PM, we would talk about how we'd failed that day. (We talked about other things too, but our failures of the day were always a critical component of our conversation.)

One might think, then, that our dinner hours were some of the most depressing and disheartening times. On the contrary, those hours were always filled with laughter, understanding, joy, questions (very few answers), hearty helpings of humility to accompany our staple white rice, and dialogue about faith, simplicity, solidarity, justice, and relationship—hours in which we examined together how we were failing, how we could be better and give more, how we could grow. These hours were a source of fuel, not only to get up the next morning and enter another day, open to grace and prepared for failure, but later became fuel for every aspect of my life thereafter. The tag line of "I fail every day" does not produce for me feelings of inadequacy or self-loathing; rather, the very honest and truthful acknowledgment that I do in fact fail every day allows me to see with more humble eyes the opportunities in which I can serve God, others, and myself more greatly with each new dawn. I am grateful for my failings.

In some ways, then, the examen of conscience offers us a chance to qualitatively evaluate, on a daily basis, our spiritual health. Journaling through the examen of conscience helps us to note patterns, to detect times of both consolation and desolation in our journey, to see each day of prayer in a larger context.

Take a few minutes now to think about your day. Think about where you can recognize God's presence in your life—where you have been able to notice God working through both your joyful and sorrowful emotions. Remember that God wants us to be happy. Embracing the happy and joyful moments of your days are just as important as recognizing where you struggle, what is a source of discontent for you, areas that require growth and attention. Think of the ways in which you have served God today and the times you have fallen short of doing so. Pray with these from a place of gratitude—thanking God for the difficult and the easy, for the happy and the sad, for the journey. As you look toward tomorrow, what might you attempt to do differently? Ask God for guidance and courage, and pray for the hope to live your faith well.

Though the basic format of the examen stays the same, we can ask varying questions within each point of prayer that will lead us into more profound reflection. Using the exact same questions every time we pray the examen can offer some sense of consistency to our days of prayer and help us more clearly see patterns in thought, prayer, behavior, and stirrings of the heart. But engaging new questions can also offer the opportunity for new directions of mind and heart that might otherwise never be elicited.

* * *

I believe we can adapt the examen of conscience to evaluate and examine our physical health as well. In some ways this would be more of an examen of conscious. *Conscience* is an inner sense of what is right and wrong, engaging one's ethics and morals into reflection and understanding of one's day and one's actions. *Conscious*, on the other hand, is more an awareness of one's surroundings, existence, and being; an awareness of what one is doing and how one is doing or performing an action.

Just as we use the points of prayer in the examen of conscience to reflect on the areas in which we have done well (served God) and the areas in which we could do better (where we have failed to serve God), we can also enter into reflection in an examen of conscious about the ways in which we have approached our health proactively—taken steps to be well and care for ourselves—and the ways in which we have failed to do so, either by omission or by approaching our health reactively.

Every day we are confronted with a number of moments in which we can make a healthy choice, good for our body and taking another step toward more wholistic health, or we can make a choice that is poor for our body. It may be as simple as choosing between doing some gardening or watching television, eating a piece of fruit or a pastry, having a glass of water or a soda. It would be helpful to engage in this reflection on our physical health daily, noting patterns and areas of potential improvement.

This examen of conscious must share the component with the examen of conscience of being rooted in gratitude—gratitude for having awakened another day, for the chance to be alive, for the opportunity to make a decision about how to care for ourselves. This examen of conscious is rooted in our giving thanks for having nutritious options at our disposal, for not relying only on what food is available rather than on what we choose; for having the ability to engage in exercise and activity in areas that are safe and comfortable; for possessing bodies capable of movement and functional performance. This gratitude for being alive serves as the basis for the reflection on our physical health—for our examen of conscious.

Let's look, then, at five points of reflection within an examen of conscious.

- Become aware of God's presence—more intentionally now in your surroundings, activity, options.
- Review the day with gratitude.
- Pay attention to your choices.
- Choose one feature of the day and pray from it.
- Look toward tomorrow.

Really, the points of reflection are virtually the same, the only slight differences being that in this area, we look for God a bit more in our physical and tangible surroundings than in our hearts and prayer, and we pay attention to our choices more than our emotions. (Although the choices we make often determine our emotions. If I choose to eat poorly and not exercise, I am much more likely to feel sluggish, lazy, and unenergized.) Being aware of the choices we make physically allows us to engage in a more proactive approach to our health. And analyzing each day where we can and should make better choices gives us the empowerment, ownership, and hopefully the willpower to make good choices for our physical health the next day, constantly striving for better.

Through this examen of conscious, we enter into thought and reflection about the tangible, physical aspects of our day: How have I used my body in a positive manner today? What have I actively done (through service to others, exercise, cleaning the house, preparing a meal) that allows my body to be a vessel of communicating God's grace and presence?

What choices have I made that contribute to my physical health and maintaining a sense of balance in my body? Have I chosen to consume food that is nutritious, full of vitamins and minerals, and nurtures my body or am I choosing food that is full of sugar and fat, that will encourage a lack of activity and a "food coma," so to speak? How much food am I consuming? Am I focused on what I need or on what I want? Do I eat until I no longer feel hungry or do

I eat until I am full? How does consuming more than what I need affect both my personal being and the state of the world at large?

Am I exercising, inviting others to join me, caring for the beautiful gift of body that God has given me? Or am I taking advantage of my health and only begin to care for myself (sleeping well, eating right, exercising) when I fall ill? How do these choices demonstrate my valuing (or devaluing) of the life God has given me, of my presence on this earth? How do these choices reflect my self-worth and appreciation for the gifts I have been given? What choices have I made today that are not as positive and healthy, and how can I be sure to make better choices tomorrow?

* * *

Our bodies are holders of the divine. As such, our examen of conscious and our examen of conscience are directly related. It is an interdependent relationship: if we begin to spend time in both examens each day, we are likely to note the correlation.

Is it difficult to note where God is present in your thoughts, emotions, spiritual life? Is it difficult to recognize moments of grace in conversations, interactions, and relationships? It might very well then be difficult to note where God is present in your movement, in your ability to perform, in your sweat and exertion. But if you can find God in a specific prayer, in a praise experience, in a cup of coffee shared with an old friend, if you can find God in witnessing a mother at the grocery store with her young child, if you can see God in the hardships of your day just as much as in the happy moments, there might be a good chance that you are more aware of God's presence in the joy of the salsa that comes on in your Zumba class, in successfully completing the tree pose in your yoga class, in feeling your feet pound the pavement in your morning run. As we witness God more clearly in our conscience-ness, we witness God more clearly in our consciousness—and vice versa.

The same goes for the other aspects of our examens. As we feel gratitude for our spiritual being, for our emotions and the ability to feel, we experience deeper appreciation for our physical presence, for the opportunity to be active and live another day on this earth, feet on the ground. Each person is blessed in unique and beautiful ways. When we have the chance to be active, to exercise regularly, to push our bodies to the next level of physical challenge—then we are very lucky.

* * *

Every time I try a new workout, a different type of exercise, I find myself experiencing a new level of gratitude. To have the opportunity to try something new, to challenge myself to improve my body in a new way, to get stronger, run faster, dance longer—these are opportunities that present themselves to me and that I choose to engage in that push me. Though being pushed can oftentimes be uncomfortable (I don't think I'll ever be comfortable, confident, or fully capable in either a CrossFit or Bikram yoga class!), it is also an opportunity for challenge, growth, and improvement for which I am very thankful. It is in those moments too in which I find myself full of gratitude for the opportunity to be exactly where I am.

When was the last time you challenged your body to do something new? When was the last time you pushed yourself to run a little farther, move your feet a little faster, jump a little higher, get in one more set of reps (lifting weights)? While it might have been difficult (and even undesirable) in the moment, were you grateful for that extra push at the end? Did you feel a new sense of accomplishment, a deeper sense of pride, a greater appreciation for your body's capability?

Very rarely have I ever gone to a CrossFit class without my friend Lou. I feel a certain level of comfort and security in knowing that

Lou is with me for that hour of what often feels like torture. While Lou is much stronger than I and we are never partnered up in class, for some reason there is a sense of security in taking on the challenge of class together. Though I often leave a CrossFit workout wanting to be stronger, better, and at times very much feeling like a failure, I am simultaneously full of thanks on many levels: that I have the opportunity to engage in difficult levels of exercise; that not only does my body have a desire to be there (and improve) but my mind has a desire to be there and be tested. Inevitably, every time I do CrossFit, at some point in the hour I think I am not going to make it. And inevitably, although I don't have the fastest time or deadlift nearly the most weight, I make it through the class and feel good at the end—that feeling of having put my whole self into it, of having expended as much power and energy as I could, of having taken one step closer to being a little faster, a little stronger, a little better. It is an exercise regime completely outside of my norm, outside of my comfort zone, and at times outside of my current capabilities. It challenges my body and mind to push further. I also notice my gratitude for Lou's presence—the companionship in challenge, the supportive presence that encourages me to try harder and push further, the sense of community that we experience in sharing the overcoming of difficult tasks.

* * *

Opportunities for gratitude abound. We need merely to be open to embracing them. In a similar fashion, we can always start anew tomorrow. When we fail to recognize God's presence (whether it be in prayer or in a workout), don't serve God as well as we could have, or treat others as less than she/he deserves, we must recognize our shortcomings but also not be paralyzed by them. As the time-less classic *Anne of Green Gables* character reminds us, "Tomorrow is always fresh, with no mistakes in it." Although we will make mistakes and we will fail, each night we have the opportunity to reflect on how we can do better tomorrow and awaken the next morning ready to make better decisions, ready to embrace gratitude more fully, ready to be healthier.

Making good decisions, making healthy choices, is like playing a game of dominoes. Once we make one unhealthy choice, it becomes so easy to continue making them. It can create a waterfall of unhealthy choices that can lead into a dark abyss. On the other hand, unfortunately, once we make one healthy choice, it doesn't continue in an easy vein to make good choices! It is difficult to make good and healthy choices; the ones that are poor for our health are much easier to fall into, right? If it were easy, everyone would do it—which makes our efforts so much more valuable in the end.

* * *

When we get into a pattern of making healthy and good choices, our lives start to become an example for others. People around us witness our choices, witness our joy, happiness, health, confidence, and the goodness with which we embrace life, and it is something to be emulated. It is a constant choice we must make, but health can be contagious—once others witness how beautiful life can be when we're healthy, they want to join! We make healthy and good decisions not only for ourselves but to bear witness to what it means to take advantage of all that God has provided to us.

Simply reflecting on our days, engaging in both the examen of conscience and the examen of conscious, is one of the best places to start as we look toward the journey of health that lies ahead. This allows us to evaluate where we are, what we do well, and what we could do better. It allows us to forge a deeper relationship with God and self, understanding more clearly how and where God is speaking to us, and where and how we need to work harder at the ways in which we live in the world. It gives us a basic outline for how we can continue to improve ourselves day after day as we work to be better servants of God, more sincere faces of Christ, as we work to treat our bodies with greater respect and make choices more conducive to both our own health and the example we set for others—thereby influencing the world for the better.

FEAR-FACTOR CHALLENGE

So where are you? Are you making good choices on a regular basis? As you examine (and examen) your days, where do you find yourself falling short time and time again? Is there a consistency to your daily struggles? Maybe you are in a very good space in your daily examen of conscious (and/or conscience). What is in place in your life that enables you to continuously make good choices? Do you have a support system that encourages you and aids you in making good choices? What if your examen of conscious isn't where you want it to be? What are some factors that might come into play with why you are unable to regularly make good choices? What keeps you from exercising regularly, eating well, spending time each day in prayer and reflection?

* * *

I have met many people over the past few years who have been afraid. Although it is by no means the case for every single person, it has been my experience that fear seems to be one of the biggest hurdles a person can be faced with, one of the biggest barriers that can be blinding. Fear can be debilitating, overwhelming, paralyzing. It can absolutely dictate everything about how we spend our days and completely influence the choices we make. Fear is a natural component to our humanity and very much a piece of most anyone's journey. A little bit of fear—conquerable fear that leads to caution—can be healthy and productive. But when the fear overwhelms us and precludes us from becoming the magnificent persons we were created to be, then we have a problem.

There have most certainly been moments in life when I was afraid. I remember going skydiving the day before my college graduation with about eight of my friends and being absolutely terrified. I was full of fear about jumping out of that plane (and truthfully, most fearful about what my mom would say if something happened and I couldn't walk across the stage the next day to receive my diploma). But with the encouragement of my friends and the fact that they conveniently "let" me board the plane last so that I had to be the first to exit, I successfully made the jump, lived to tell the tale, and receive my diploma. I had been scared, but I trusted my friends and the man with whom I jumped tandem and overcame the fear.

There have been moments when I have found myself in precarious situations during my traveling and living abroad in areas of stark economic depression and have felt fear. Fortunately, despite the gravity of some of these situations, I made it through—whether it was due to the protection of the Holy Spirit, a guardian angel watching over me, the support of others around me, or my own decision to swallow my fear and move through it. I came out on the other side—stronger, more capable, I would like to think slightly wiser, and definitely feeling more confident of handling whatever the world might throw at me next. Moving through the fear is what has gotten me to a place of being cautious but not afraid. There is a big difference, and I will get back to this shortly.

In my work within health and fitness, I often see people who are afraid. Over the years many people have said to me, "I am afraid to try a Zumba class. I have no rhythm!" I have had people look at me like I'm crazy during a personal-training session when I explain what exercise we will be doing next. When I ask why they are looking at me like that, they very clearly state, "I can't do that." "Oh no?" I respond. "Have you ever tried?" "Well, no," he/she says, "but it looks scary." Sometimes it's not even in a work capacity but when I invite someone to join me for a group fitness class or a run. "I can't do that. I won't be able to keep up with you. I won't make it through that class. I'm scared."

Although fear is a real emotion in these cases, I have to question its validity. When the fear is caused/followed by the statement, "I can't do that," I sense that it is more than likely a false fear. How do you know you can't do something if you have never tried? Now, if you try and it doesn't work, then we modify. We change whatever it is while still pushing you out of your comfort zone, challenging your body a bit more, requiring a bit more physical effort than you are used to.

Or maybe it means we start small and work our way up—what we call the training principle of progression. But it is not meant to be an insurmountable barrier. I get frustrated when fear keeps someone from trying, from making even one attempt, because it's grounded, I believe, in selfishness—selfishness in that we don't try because we don't want to fail. We'd rather continue in our comfort zone, continue not pushing ourselves to do more, be better, be challenged more because it's uncomfortable when we do. But we are not called to be complacent beings who are comfortable. We are called to be uncomfortable, to be at dis-ease, to be challenged, and to challenge. To remain comfortable is to be selfish.

* * *

I had a client once who possessed great potential. She would make a decision to get in shape, and for weeks she would train hard, eat right, stop drinking as much, stop going out as much, sleep more, see results, and be doing excellently. And then she would stop—working out, going to Zumba classes regularly, making healthy food/nutrient choices. And of course, the weight loss and muscle gaining would stop. This would be cyclical. I would see her and challenge her to try something new—start running, try CrossFit, attend a yoga class. She always had an excuse, a reason not to. I knew deep down that she was afraid, but this fear manifested through any number of different reasons and excuses to avoid pushing herself. She would still come to Zumba class, though much less regularly, but that was about it. She was not on a track to healthy weight loss or to taking care of herself. She is a magnificent person, with so much potential and so much goodness to give to this world, but she lacks confidence in who she is and what she is capable of. She doesn't care for herself as she should or make the best decisions; she is afraid—of what exactly, I am not 100 percent sure, but I imagine failure or perhaps embarrassment. This approach to health is a very selfish one.

When we focus on what we want based solely on our human desires—to go out a lot, to indulge in sweet things or alcohol, to watch television instead of exercising—rather than taking into account what will help us be better prepared to serve the world and fulfill the call God has placed on our hearts, we are being selfish. When we focus on our individual comfort zones versus what invites us to build community and walk with others on a common journey (even if, and especially when, it is a journey of struggle and progression), we are being selfish. When we care more about indulgences and instant gratification as opposed to what will keep us around and healthy for our families, friends, and communities, we are being selfish. In many ways, neglecting our physical health is an extremely selfish approach to life.

Indeed, by neglecting our physical health, we are neglecting God—we are choosing not to honor the divine within us as it deserves, we are placing more emphasis and importance on ourselves (wants, desires) than on the needs of others, and we are very much taking the easy way out. Now, this is not to say that everyone who is in an unhealthy state, who is overweight, sedentary, or makes poor food choices is happy with the space they are in or the state of their health. In fact, more often than not, they are not happy; not many people desire to be overweight, obese, and/or inactive. However, by continuing to let ourselves settle in this space, we are indulging this selfishness.

If we can come to recognize this dwelling of our bodies and spirits in a place of selfishness, a huge hurdle has already been jumped. It is never easy to admit our failings; it calls for extreme humility, for recognizing our raw and broken humanness, for seeing that we have failed to look outside ourselves. This is not easy, but it is necessary for change. If we allow our health to be determined by overindulgence, by a lack of confidence, and/or by a desire to stay within our comfort zones and refuse to look beyond these, we are limiting ourselves—we become confined by fear and stay stagnant in this selfish space. Does this resonate with you at all? It is a difficult admission to make; but again, know that you are not alone. Oftentimes, when we realize that our actions are not only harming us but also neglecting (and at times even harming) God and important persons in our lives, it can serve as a wake-up call to seriously consider and reevaluate why we are in the space we are in.

Of course, many factors come into play with one's physical health—natural limitations/disabilities, family history/genetics, cultural/socioeconomic implications, and many others. But those of us who have access to healthy food, to exercise, and to the ability to *choose health* and still don't make that choice—are selfish and irresponsible and failing to live God's call for us as one human family. To remain within our comfort zone of dis-ease, especially when access to health is at our fingertips, is rooted in this selfishness and arrogance; fear is not a valid reason not to overcome, not to challenge ourselves to grow.

* * *

Fear can also be applied to our spiritual journeys. At times we fear that to which God is calling us will inevitably call us well outside our comfort zone, challenge us to see our faith and the world in new ways, move outside of what we know and have experienced to something new, different, greater. It will likely challenge us to change and grow and reflect and enter deeply into the stirrings of our heart and a discernment of spirits.

We are often afraid of that to which God is calling us because in many ways, we will have to embrace a vocation, a spirit, a role in this world that might not be "normal," that might be contrary to the status quo or what society dictates should be the next step. I think about this often when I think of two people who have both recently discerned and answered the call to religious life.

These two women, dear friends of mine, are beautiful, magnificent females who have so much to give to this world. They have enormous hearts, a faith that inspires, a profound sense of self, a belief in a world that is better than the one in which we currently live, a desire to serve others that is unparalleled by the common person. Not only are they both beautiful on the inside, but their inner beauty is matched by their physical, outward beauty as well. Both have received questions throughout their discernment as to why they feel the need to be a nun. Both have expressed a desire to have a family, bear children, experience romantic love and relationship. Their decision to enter religious life is not a common occurrence these days and, as they share with me, brings certain levels of fear and questioning. Why is God calling them to this life? Will they be fulfilled in this vocation for the rest of their lives? Will religious community fill their hearts "enough"? Will they have the courage to live without physical touch and affection and expressions of romantic love from a partner? How will they continue to respond to the reaction of much of society—the questioning, the sense that a young woman "should" get married and have children, the challenge of very much taking a road less traveled?

These magnificent women, who have chosen to fully embrace the call God has placed on their hearts, certainly serve for me a bold and remarkable example of courage, of indescribable faith, of selflessness in some of its most powerful forms. These women, with whom I am blessed to know and share time, space, and this journey, are modern-day prophets. They speak a truth through their lives and commitment to faith that sets an inspiring example of selflessness and trust.

We are all called to be prophets in our own unique way. We are created for greatness; to bring change to our world; to be examples of a better, more just way of life; to live in search of truth and our vocation; to be for others, with others. We are created to not be fearful, to live honoring our spirits and hearts regardless of what society tells us is the "normal" or "right" path. We are created to care for our bodies so that we can best use them in service to others; to recognize and feed the divine within us; to be healthy and proactive individuals, fighting for a better tomorrow for all who inhabit our earth. We are created to grow and move through our fears and to give of our lives in the manner and to the magnitude to which God invites and challenges us.

Of what are you afraid? Are you afraid of becoming the person God has in mind? Why? Do you fear trying something new that will be difficult but may very well be worth the fight? What keeps you remaining in your comfort zone, whether it is physically or spiritually? Can you recognize some selfishness within you? Is this prohibiting you from serving your loved ones, others, your community, God, and yourself to the extent of which you are capable? Are you currently living in a state of injustice—a disconnect in your relationship with yourself, with God, and with others? How do you raise your prophetic voice? Where do you find examples of selflessness and courage in your life? Are you an example of this? Why not? Do you want to be? How can you become that example? What is keeping you from being the best you possible?

* * *

There is a very fine line between being cautious and being afraid. It can, at times, be very difficult to know the difference. All too often we disguise what is really fear as caution (or convince ourselves it's caution) purely for the desire to stay in our comfort zone. But the difference between fear and caution, though a fine line, is significant. We can look at caution and fear and again make the distinction between living and existing, between living for others or living for ourselves. We need to come to understand when to have the courage to push ourselves beyond what is comfortable and easy and challenge ourselves to be healthier, to work toward wholeness, and when we are using caution as an excuse for an unfounded fear, trying to justify remaining in a place that is not healthy (physically and/or spiritually).

Given the world we live in, with danger, violence, the frequency of people making mistakes, egoism, selfishness, power struggles, and so forth, it is not a bad thing to be cautious. Things can happen anywhere, to anyone—being on our toes, making good decisions about the company we keep, the places we go, and how we choose to spend our time are all smart ways of being in the world. However, if we start making decisions based on the fear of what "might" happen, if we stay so narrowly in our comfort zones to avoid challenge and change, we can easily fall into a place of paralysis—so much so that we cease to live.

* * *

When I moved to Ecuador, I did not know the culture, the language, the people, or the societal norms. It would have been very easy for me to quickly become afraid, especially living in an area that struggled severely with economic poverty, where drug and alcohol addiction was rampant, where weapons were frequently owned and used. I could easily have fallen into a life of fear, and had that been the case, I really wouldn't have lived my experience there at all. There might even be some people who would have expected me to live a life of fear. I was often asked in correspondence from people at home in the U.S. if I was afraid, if I was targeted, what the chances were of my being put in a dangerous situation. And truth be told, there were dangerous situations around and many times when I could have chosen to give in to fear. But that happens anywhere; living in fear is a choice I have as much on Long Island as in Ecuador. Although economic and societal situations at times affect the way a community lives and how people use or abuse power or violence, it can happen anywhere. But living a life of fear—trusting no one, constantly questioning others' motives, doubting our own capability, doubting God's guiding presence that cares for and protects us—is certainly not a healthy way to live.

So instead I chose (and continue to choose) a life that includes caution but not fear. I am specific about whom I associate with, where I hang out, what I indulge in (and to what extent), where I go alone, and whom I trust. Does this always keep me safe and exempt from bad things? Absolutely not. To be honest, I have found myself in undesirable situations at times. Would those things not have occurred had I been living in fear? Maybe. Maybe if I was constantly fearful and avoided putting myself and my heart on the line, I wouldn't get hurt. But I also likely wouldn't be enjoying much of anything in life, and I certainly wouldn't be living up to my potential, nor would I be living authentically. And I have to trust that when those undesirable situations occur and I discover a way to grow through them, there is a strong presence of grace. I don't take this to mean that "everything happens for a reason," but rather, that from every situation we have a chance to grow and learn and see manifestations of God at work. This grace allows me to use these experiences—even if difficult or at times harmful—to better serve others, to know God more closely, and to get to know myself in a new (and often stronger) way.

Fear does not allow us to live a healthy life—so much so that it can invade and inhibit every dimension of health as we know it. Fear keeps us from being the people God calls us to be and affects our social relationships and interactions. Fear keeps us from achieving stable levels of physical fitness, interferes with the environment we create, prevents us from seeing ourselves in a positive light and how we react to the world around us. It affects the level of challenge and growth we engage in mentally and theoretically and how we handle stress and change. Fear does not create an atmosphere in which we can be our best possible selves, and living in fear does not allow fully for embracing health and happiness, for being well and whole.

* * *

At multiple times throughout this book, I have talked about different visions of what healthy and unhealthy look like—from finding our passion to serving others, to living in fear, to being in community, to exercising and eating a balanced diet, and to many other aspects of physical and spiritual health and wellness. As with any concrete program that tends to be life-altering, one of the biggest steps toward change is to recognize and admit being in a state where health is lacking—a state of dis-ease.

Maybe it means you are not at ease (and by *ease* here, I mean confident that you are healthy, happy, and well) with your spiritual life. You are experiencing that place of desolation—a lack of fulfillment, a lack of desire to pray and be in communion with others, not a strong sense of purpose, a real questioning of God's presence and hand, feeling disconnected from community, lacking spiritual energy, lacking a vision for that which is greater than the here and now.

Or maybe you are at dis-ease in regards to physical health—you don't have the energy to exercise regularly or perhaps even have the energy needed to complete the day's tasks without feeling tired and run down. Perhaps you don't fuel your body with nutrient-rich foods that prevent you from feeling hungry or constantly caffeinated and jittery. You don't feel like you are capable of much physical exertion; you are not fully content with your strength, endurance, or ability to complete moderate physical tasks. You experience a lack of desire to proactively take steps toward attaining and maintaining a sound space of health.

In some cases, maybe it's both. Perhaps both your physical and spiritual self is being challenged and you are experiencing all of the above. This can be an unbelievably difficult place to be—feeling lost, struggling to feel like you belong (in a specific community, in your vocation, in this time and place), not having the wherewithal or the desire to constantly push yourself toward more. That feeling can be numbing to the point of incapacitation; you shut down, start to go through only the absolutely necessary motions without much thought, without any energy, without any sort of conviction for who you are, what you're doing, or why you're doing it. You become unbelievably stagnant and feel on some days like you are slowly sinking in quicksand.

It's an ugly place to be—spiritually and/or physically unhealthy and diseased. At some point I hope that something makes you realize you can't live like this anymore. Maybe it's something you read in this book; maybe it's a comment of concern from a loved one; maybe it's a doctor's mandate to change your current lifestyle. Whatever it is, I hope and pray that if you are in this place, something clicks. But perhaps you have searched—tried different diets, exercise, forms of prayer, worshiping communities—and nothing has clicked. The spark hasn't been lit yet. If that is the case—if you know you need to change but have yet to find the one thing that pushes you over the edge enough to engage in change—then I would encourage you to find someone to talk with on a regular basis. Whether it be a counselor, a spiritual director, a life coach, or a wellness consultant, find someone you can talk to regularly who can offer you the companionship and accountability you need to move toward change, who can offer new insight (especially if you are stuck on the fact that you have this desire to change but cannot successfully start and continue the process). You might need that extra support and accompaniment, and if you (with outside support) can find the courage to make this move toward health before something drastic happens, the better off you will be. Because coming out of this unhealthy state, though difficult, is a magnificent (albeit long and at times quite arduous) journey. But once you reach the other side—which will require amazing diligence and commitment—you can appreciate the human journey so much more and truly give of yourself to accompany others in that same search.

Amidst the difficulty, there is hope. We, as Catholics, are a people of hope—a resurrection people who believe that the paschal mystery is alive and well in our world. Hope is a virtue quite different from the emotion of optimism, and it is by and through hope that we have the strength to search for and respond to God's presence on this earth. But it takes time and patience and dedication. The Spanish language, in all its wisdom, uses the same exact word for the verb "to hope" and the verb "to wait": *esperar*. The same word has two meanings that, in English, we might often use in very distinct situations, but in Spanish, it is the same word. There is wisdom in that fact: we must wait actively, proactively, intentionally, and intently, hoping for the new life that is to come. There is hope for each one of us to be healthy, happy, whole, and well; to find our passions and let them lead us to freedom; and to let this cycle continue in us down a never-ending (although winding and tricky at times) path.

* * *

On December 2, 1980, four churchwomen were murdered by government troops in El Salvador as they served as missionaries during some of the most tumultuous and dangerous years in Latin American history. These women are examples for us of prophets, of courageous believers, and of livers and doers of the Word of God. One of them, Ita Ford, MM, is well known for these words she left in a letter to her niece:

"I hope you come to find that which gives life a deep meaning for you. Something worth living for—maybe even worth dying for—something that energizes you, enthuses you, enables you to keep moving ahead."

Ita was really on to something here—encouraging her niece to find that passion that would lead her to a healthy place and a place of freedom.

* * *

You're likely to have heard at some point the simple and well-known truth spoken by the Chinese philosopher Lao-Tzu, "The journey of a thousand miles begins with a single step." The same is true for the journey toward health (happiness and wholeness). In many ways, it is a thousand-mile journey, for it is never ending. No matter when we reach that place of health and freedom (which we all can and will reach if we dedicate ourselves to it), we will constantly have to work at maintaining what has taken such great effort to achieve. And the journey of maintenance is even longer than the journey of obtainment. But it begins with just one step—one choice, one decision—that leads to step after step, choice after choice that is healthy, passion-driving, and freeing.

Finding others to walk the journey with you will help. Finding sources of support, encouragement, and accompaniment will give you strength. Finding healthy coping mechanisms will help when you fall off the wagon. Recording and calling to mind successes will help you get back on the wagon. Allowing yourself to eat a piece of dark chocolate, have a glass of wine, splurge on a piece of sweetbread, give yourself a day off from journaling and exercise will all help you to maintain balance. Staying away for the most part from chocolate, not drinking anything to excess, limiting sugar intake, journaling, and exercising will help you maintain your health.

The journey is long—lifelong. It is also challenging, beautiful, grace-filled, and so worth it. It has to start somewhere, it has to start someday—so what are you afraid of? Why not now, why not today?

A FEW RECIPES

Now, I'm sure that by this point in the book you have undoubtedly had a complete spiritual awakening and epiphany about the revival of your health and have already begun the transformation to a new and better you, right? It's that easy, isn't it? Read a few pages, recognize that on which you could be working a little harder and on which you could spend a bit more attention and to which you could be dedicating a bit more time. As easy as the flip of a page, you can turn your life around and catapult your health into a brand-new category of completeness, wholeness, happiness, wellness. Simple as pie...hmmm, pie. Yum! There goes my focus on healthy food choices.

OK, maybe it's not that easy. We can still very quickly get distracted at the thought of delicious desserts, curling up in bed instead of going for a run, watching *So You Think You Can Dance* instead of trying out our own skills and moves in the Zumba studio (and perhaps tricking ourselves into thinking we just might have what it takes to move from *So You Think You Can Dance* to *Dancing With the Stars*). We can still become complacent, apathetic, self-doubting, fearful, and selfish. We are constantly surrounded by that which tempts us, taunts us, invites us into the easy, into the comfort zone, into the selfish, into the status quo, into the reactive approach, into the safety net void of exploration, void of discovery, void of passion, void of freedom—void of true health. But at least now, we have a slightly better idea of what we can achieve and what we need to become more fully the persons God has created us to be. All that's left is honing in on our personal, specific path and walking it.

Still, the whole thought of redirecting our journey of health can, understandably, be somewhat intimidating. Let's see if we can break it down a bit—reinforce a few tangible, realistic how-to items that might get us on the right track and make the whole picture seem a little less frightening.

* * *

Let's start by breaking down an approach to greater physical health. Something very basic that we can do easily is to surround ourselves with positive thoughts—words that offer encouragement and motivation. Some of them might air on the bit more cheesy side that we in the fitness industry tend to use—a lot! For example, "It doesn't matter how fast you run. You're lapping everyone on the couch!" or "Nothing tastes as good as being fit feels!" Others might be very simple truths but ones we often have a hard time remembering on a daily basis: "Today you have the option to be better than you were yesterday." "Every journey begins with a single step, but you'll never finish if you don't start." Others might be less vague and a bit more cut-throat, if you will: "There's no reason for you to not exercise today. None. Get your lazy butt moving." (Consider it a little bit of tough self-love.)

Each one of us is different and responds to different stimuli and motivation. While some may need more affirmation, others might need a bit more harshness to get moving. Only you can know what you will respond to and what will propel you to make good choices and get motivated. Once you have your words selected, put them in a place where you are bound to see them every day and, preferably, where you will see them when you are in that "I know I should work out but I really don't want to" mental space. For example, if you are a morning person and are much more likely to exercise in the morning, grab a washable marker (or an eye-liner/lip-liner pencil, for that matter) and write your chosen words on the bathroom mirror. When you wake up in the morning, you'll see these words, and it might make the difference as to whether you go for a run that morning. If you are a "I'm much more likely to work out after work" person, add a sticky note to your desktop background/monitor so that you are bound to read those words as you shut off your computer and leave work for the day. Maybe you are attached to your cell phone. Make these words your banner when you turn on your phone, or (if you really want to guilt yourself into doing exercise) make one choice word your password to unlock your phone (exercise, Zumba, weight loss, healthy). These might sound like silly little things, but they make a world of difference—at least they have in my experience. When I have been in tough spaces and have felt incredibly unmotivated, I have used these tricks (in fact, I have done almost all of the above at some point). Little things make a big difference.

Throughout this book I have talked about the importance of moral support, of accompaniment and accountability. This is another set of ways to encourage your journey toward greater physical health. The old adage "misery loves company" holds some truth (though I would argue that once you get to your place of passion and freedom—and health—exercise is significantly less miserable). We all have friends who want to lose weight, be healthier, push themselves a little further. Ask a friend to serve as an accountability partner. Set a goal of working out together three times a week or committing to running a 5K after three months of training.

About a year and a half ago, I was not running at all. One of the girls in my Zumba class asked if I'd be interested in running a half marathon. She had never run one before, and doing so was one of her life goals. We began training together, meeting up once a week to do our long runs early on Sunday mornings. This woman quickly became one of my good friends as we spent hours running together each weekend. Knowing she was waiting for me at our starting path each Sunday kept me from cutting out on a run. I never would have gotten into running again had it not been for her invitation and our relationship of accountability—which then, unexpectedly, made room for a friendship to grow.

The weekend of the half marathon, as we "carb loaded" together the night before (which really is a fitness myth in regards to long-distance running, but that's another story) and met up that fateful Sunday morning in November, I had never been more grateful for our shared experience of training and then completing our goal. What a gift that journey became. Working out with an account-ability partner provides not only someone to ensure you show up to exercise, someone to share in the journey, someone to (at times) share in the misery, but also someone to share in the amazing feeling of reaching a goal—someone who will support you and celebrate with you, push you to be better, and—if you're lucky—someone who just might be an understanding friend and source of companionship.

Perhaps you are a person who can't self-motivate—perhaps you need someone to tell you what to do. Hiring a personal trainer can be very beneficial for those who don't want to or can't spend the time thinking about what exercises to do, in what order, to what extent, and so forth. By hiring a trainer, we eliminate the ownership of figuring out and designing an exercise routine. We simply show up, and the trainer tells us exactly what to do and how to do it—a big benefit, especially if we are new to the fitness world. Oftentimes people think they can go to a gym and use machines or buy hand weights and figure it out, and their form will be completely incor-rect. Not only will you not gain the benefits you desire, but you might actually do more harm than good to your body if you are performing exercises incorrectly.

If you do decide to hire a trainer, be sure to meet with and in-terview the person before signing a contract. First and foremost, make sure the trainer is certified and knowledgeable. If he/she does not have a certification from a national fitness organization, you might want to look for someone else. (Since the requirements for trainers vary across the nation, even some gyms/clubs don't require their trainers to be certified. Be sure your trainer can provide information on where and when he/she became certified.)

Another big piece of working with a trainer is determining if personality is a good fit. You need someone who will mesh well with your needs, goals, desires, and personality. If you despise running and wind up with a trainer who only makes clients run, then it's probably not a good fit. You need a trainer who will motivate you but who also knows how to set achievable goals and help you get there. If you desire to tone up and slim down and in the first session your trainer is talking about you competing in the next city boxing match, it might not be the best fit. Don't be afraid to ask questions, get to know the person a bit, and have conversations with multiple trainers until you find someone who fits you. Hiring a personal trainer is a big investment of time, money, and trust in another person's ability to guide your fitness journey; it's not something to be taken lightly.

Probably one of the more important components to developing a physical-fitness/workout routine that you enjoy is finding an exercise that relates to your likes. For example, if you enjoy being outside, find a weekend walking club at the local park. If you enjoy dancing, try a Zumba or belly-dancing class. If you prefer to be in your own head and use your exercise time as prayer time, find a good trail to walk or run that is not overly populated. If you like being told what to do and pushed harder, consider a personal trainer. If you thrive on competition, you might want to test out a CrossFit class. If sweating makes you feel accomplished, check out a Bikram yoga class in your area. If you want to get your heart rate up but have had some knee problems and can't handle much high impact, you might look for a spinning class.

You get the idea. Decide what your needs are and what you enjoy, and then look for that which might correspond. Not sure what kind of exercise you might enjoy? Then perhaps you might want to sign up for a trial period at a gym that offers an array of various classes and try multiple ones before committing to a Zumba studio or CrossFit gym. One of the key components in this is not to be afraid to try new things. In every class, we instructors were once in your spot. I remember how scared I was to take my first Zumba class, not having any idea what to expect, and I was a mess! I could barely follow a step and had no idea what I was doing. And because I remember how that felt, I have no problem challenging others to try it at least once. You'll never know what amazing gifts can become available if you just try something.

* * *

We can take a similar approach to our spiritual health. Start with the small things: find just ten minutes a day to spend in prayer. This doesn't necessarily mean that you need to take ten minutes away from something you are already doing, but rather, refocus yourself during a daily task, like using your shower time as intentional prayer time. Or instead of listening to music on the way to work in the morning, turn off the radio for the first ten minutes of your commute and chitchat with God a bit. Perhaps instead of spending a full lunch hour socializing and eating, you finish your food in fifty minutes and spend the last ten taking a walk outside and being quiet in prayer. These are simple options to slightly revamp tasks you already do, and you don't even need to squeeze another ten minutes out of your (likely already very busy) daily routine.

When I lived in Ecuador, I had an amazing gift of time. We, of course, worked and held responsibilities at different programs, schools, ministries, and so forth, but the gift of time and never being rushed was something I valued deeply. (That proves next to impossible for me in this crazy First-World culture of impatience and hurriedness in which I now find myself.) Every morning for a year during my time there, I woke up and spent an hour journaling. Spending that hour every day capturing my prayers, my hopes, my struggles, and the movements of my heart on paper was my prayer time. Only one of my six housemates awoke at the same time I did, and we spent that hour together in silence each morning. We drank our coffee and ate a piece of bread, and there was more significant companionship in that hour of silence than in most other moments of conversation in community throughout a typical day. I cherished those hours, and now, looking back, I cherish them even more; they were some of the most formative times of prayer I have ever had.

Now, I am not saying that everyone has to spend an hour journaling each morning. Lord knows, I certainly don't in my current lifestyle, jobs, and schedule. But the act of journaling prayer stays with me, and though I don't practice it as frequently as I would like, I crave and take advantage of those moments when I am able to engage in such prayer. Have you ever journaled? If not, I strongly suggest you try it. But keep in mind that a journal is not a diary; don't let it become a litany of the things you did that day (or the day before) and the people you saw. Let your heart write. Record your thoughts, dreams, the challenges and the emotions that accompany those challenges. Offer in writing your prayers and what you ask God for and what you need from God to be a better, more complete person. Let your writing be your prayer.

Perhaps you're not a writer or an introvert. Maybe you find yourself closest to God with other people, in conversation and sharing, and get your energy from being with others. If so, have you thought about finding a faith-sharing group or a prayer group? Check with your local parish or the ministry office at a nearby Catholic university. Maybe you can find a group of people who get together on a regular basis—once a month, twice a month, even weekly—and read Scripture or faith-based passages and discuss it. Some parishes offer formal programs. (JustFaith is one such group that meets weekly to reflect on the connection between faith and social justice and our roles in the world. Check with your local parish to see if it offers the program.)

Or perhaps you can find a more informal group of adults who get together and read Sunday's gospel and then spend some time discussing how it connects to their lives. This can be amazingly fruitful, especially with a group of people who come from various backgrounds and who are open to sharing their life experiences. It is also very much rooted in one of the forms of Church celebrated in the Latino culture—comunidad base, where Church is very much groups of people in often materially poor areas gathering at night to read Scripture and share homilies, since they often had to work the fields during the time Mass was offered. It is a beautiful form of prayer that can be amazingly rich when entered into with an open heart and mind.

If you need something a bit more formal, you might seek out opportunities for adoration of the Blessed Sacrament or a book with the Liturgy of the Hours (from the ministry of Divine Office) that will allow you to open up to night prayer and offer it before you go to sleep. These prayer experiences are a bit more structured and might work better for those who (much like when working with a personal trainer) prefer to be told what to do. Praying the Liturgy of the Hours gives you prayers—words and offerings laid out in print—that guide you through morning and/or night prayer. This can be a beautiful form of prayer for some Catholics, particularly as we recognize that people from all walks of life within our faith tradition offer the same exact prayers. To pray the Liturgy of the Hours, knowing that Catholics around the world are using the same words to engage more fully in their relationship with God in a variety of languages, countries, and cultural situations can be a powerful experience of community and shared praise. The Liturgy of the Hours uses Scripture, and particularly the psalms, to harmonize one's voice and heart and unite one to the larger Catholic community in our world. Praying the Liturgy of the Hours often flows into a practice of *lectio divina*, which is sitting and meditating with Scripture passages in a way that allows the Word of God to enter our hearts and lives in a more personal manner. Your local parish and/or archdiocesan offices should have resources and information on praying the Liturgy of the Hours.

Another opportunity that might be worth pursuing is finding a spiritual director. A spiritual director is a person trained in the task of accompanying another on his/her spiritual journey, of asking questions that will lead one to greater clarity, greater discovery, and greater relationship with God. Spiritual directors shouldn't be confused with counselors or psychologists. They are certainly there to listen to your struggles and offer insight from an often more developed spiritual background, but the focus is on your relationship with God and helping you get to the next step of your spiritual journey and awakening.

Spiritual direction can be a magnificent opportunity, and oftentimes spiritual directors have an incredibly gentle yet firm way of telling us what we need to hear—and in a way that will make us want to actually listen. Much like a personal trainer, the right spiritual director has to be a good match of experience and personality and, I would add, a mesh of prayer styles. For example, as someone whose foundation for prayer life is very much rooted in Ignatian spirituality, with a flavor of Marianist charism to complement— two spiritual traditions that are very active, very people-oriented, and very relational and a profound experience of God in the Latino culture—my best option for a spiritual director would probably be someone who has an understanding of a smattering of these, perhaps someone who has done missionary work abroad, studied at a Jesuit university, or understands the concept of sodalities. (Father Chaminade, founder of the Marianist Order, believed in the power of sodalities: a group of people coming together in communion to pray and share as a means to change the world.) I need to find someone whose style and personality and spirituality fits mine, but who will also challenge me to go further and grow more in my own journey.

Similar to one's fitness journey, our spiritual path also requires that we take small steps. Perhaps the idea of committing to meet with a spiritual director on a regular basis is too much right now. Your first step might be as simple as signing up for an online daily reflection. There are plenty out there (some of my favorites are from the Henri Nouwen Society and Richard Rohr). You can submit your e-mail address and each morning you will find a reflection waiting in your inbox (one of the joys of technology). Or you can proactively spend a few minutes each day accessing a website where you can read the day's gospel or read the gospel accompanied by a reflection. (I love Creighton University's Online Ministry daily readings and reflection.) Perhaps you can start by reading one or two reflections a week and sitting with it for a day or two. After a month of that, perhaps you increase and read three or four reflections a week—maybe from the same source if you are getting something out of it, or maybe you diversify. Start slow, and build your way up.

* * *

I have found that the best way to actually commit to something is to name it. By that I mean having specific, tangible, obtainable steps to help you reach your goal(s). So here's the "let's make it happen for real" portion of this book. Take out your journal (or a piece of paper or flip to the inside back cover of this book—whatever works for you) and write down three things you can—and *will*—do over the course of the next month to move forward in your health and wellness journey. Use examples I have given or come up with your own, but write down three things you can commit to doing in the coming weeks to start making a life change. Remember, transformation is not going to happen overnight by any means, but you have to start somewhere. Where will you start?

* * *

In both our physical and spiritual journeys toward health and wellness, taking small steps that offer both challenge and opportunities for growth, as well as some comfort in meeting ourselves where we are, are of utmost importance. But it will not happen overnight, and we cannot expect dramatic changes in an unreasonably short period of time. We often hear that "patience is a virtue." Indeed it is, and we must know how to be patient with ourselves as we embark upon new stages of our journey. Try not to get frustrated with yourself if progress is slow, as long as you can honestly say you are working hard, staying committed, and making an effort. It will take time, and as we talked about early on, there really is no "end point" on our path to health and wellness. There may be times of progress and times of maintenance, times to focus on one dimension of health more than another, times when we need to pay attention more actively to one area or another. But it is a never-ending journey, full of challenge and struggle, some failure to be sure, but also full of grace, joy, success, and happiness.

* * *

I cannot promise that in six months or a year, you will be different. I cannot promise that you will be twenty pounds lighter, have a better relationship with God, that you will know and understand yourself better, or that you will find your passion or experience great freedom. The strength, conviction, capacity to change, and ability to achieve that great freedom is within you and you alone, and no amount of advice or personal insight from me will get you where you want and need to be unless you make a very clear choice to change.

What I can promise is that you are not alone. Not only are there others (at least, there is someone!) out there who understand and can empathize with your journey, but in any moment and all moments, we are accompanied by the greatest friend we can have: our God. First, find solace in community—even if it is with individuals you may never meet personally or with whom you form an intimate relationship. Allow the fact that you are not alone to be of comfort and refuge to you. Second, spend some time thinking about the person of God with whom you best relate. Maybe it is God the Father, maybe it is Sophia Wisdom as the Holy Spirit, maybe it is Jesus as the Son of God. Maybe you most relate to Mary as mother/sister/friend. Just as you are drawn to certain people in friendship because of how well you relate to them, discern who it is you feel most comfortable praying to and sharing with. Our Creator is always with us: trust that fact.

THAT'S A WRAP!

I truly hope that your experience of reading, reflecting, thinking, and praying through this book has been a positive one. Together we have walked a journey of recognition, of self-disclosure, of greater awareness and understanding about who you are, where you are, who you want to be, and where you can be. We have delved deeply into the interconnectedness of the various dimensions of our health, but most specifically our physical and spiritual beings. We have discerned passions and laid out the path from focusing on one dimension's passion leading to our health, to our freedom, and the empowerment to then be released into the next dimension. You have tools at your fingertips to help you examine and engage; you have options of where to find a community of support and accountability.

I want to remind you that this journey is continuous. There is no clear end point, no time when you will say, "OK, I'm done, I'm healthy; I don't have to worry about it or focus on it anymore." You will always need to focus, always need to be aware of yourself, always need to continue making positive, healthy choices to stay on the path to wellness.

Remember that our health is synonymous with justice: we are striving for right relationship with God, self, and others. Justice is achievable, but it requires effort, attention, and commitment. Justice is attainable, but it demands a willingness to surrender, a dying to self, an understanding of who we are, who God is, and who the world is—all of us as one human family, striving for beauty and goodness, striving for health and happiness. Justice is within our reach—we must take that first step to make possible what we may otherwise consider impossible. We must spend time getting to know ourselves, getting to know God, getting to know one another. We are on this journey together; be encouraged in your search.

Finally, I offer you comfort and companionship in the promise of my prayers. I promise you that I am holding you in prayer, that I am asking the Holy Spirit to accompany and encourage you, the Blessed Mother to inspire and infuse you with her grace, and that you find deep passion and freedom, happiness, wellness, health, and wholeness. I promise you that when my feet move and my heart swells through a blasting salsa and a loaded merengue, I am moving in prayer for you to find great joy and success in this journey toward a better life and a healthier, freer you.

See you on the dance floor!

SOURCES

Coburn, Jared W., and Malek, Moh H. NSCA's *Essentials of Personal Training: Second Edition.* Champaign, IL: Human Kinetics, 2012.

Klavora, Peter. *Foundations of Kinesiology: Studying Human Movement and Health: Second Edition.* Toronto, ON, Canada: Sport Books Publisher, 2011.

Nouwen, Henri J., *¡Gracias!* Maryknoll, NY: Orbis Books, 2002.

Renfrew Center Foundation for Eating Disorders. "Eating Disorders 101 Guide: A Summary of Issues, Statistics and Resources, 2003." National Association of Anorexia Nervosa and Associated Disorders, Inc. Available at anad.org/get-information/about-eating-disorders/eating-disorders-statistics/.

Untener, Bishop Ken, of Saginaw, Michigan. "Prophets of a Future Not Our Own." Available at usccb.org/prayer-and-worship/prayers/archbishop_romero_prayer.cfm.